Contents

Abbreviations used in the text

ACP African, Caribbean and Pacific countries
ALADI Latin American Integration Association
AMS Aggregate Measure of Support
ASEAN Association of South East Asian Nations
CACM Central American Integration Agreements
CAP Common Agricultural Policy
CEEC Central and Eastern European Countries
EEA European Economic Area
EFTA European Free Trade Association
EU European Union
FDI Foreign Direct Investment
FSU Former Soviet Union
FTA Free Trade Agreement
GATS General Agreement on Trade in Services
GATT General Agreement on Tariffs and Trade
GDP Gross Domestic Product
GNP Gross National Product
GSP Generalised System of Preferences
HS Harmonised Commodity Description and Coding System
IMF International Monetary Fund
LDDC Least-Developed Developing Country
Mercosur Common Market of the South
MFA Multifibre Arrangement
MFN Most Favoured Nation
NAFTA North American Free Trade Agreement
NIE Newly Industrialising Economy
OECD Organisation for Economic Co-operation and Development
REPA Regional Economic Partnership Agreement
RW Rest of the world
SACU Southern African Customs Union
SEM Single European Market
TRIMS Trade-Related Investment Measures
TRIPS Trade-Related Aspects of Intellectual Property Rights
WTO World Trade Organization

Executive Summary

This report has been prepared to assist the African, Caribbean and Pacific countries (ACP) to develop a detailed strategy for their relationship with the European Union (EU) after the expiry of the Lomé Convention. It aims to provide a contribution both to the current negotiations and to appropriate policy formation within ACP countries.

The report is based on the premise that a continuation of the status quo in terms of effective as opposed to nominal access to the European market is not an option. This is because forces operating outside the Convention will undermine Lomé preferences if the relationship is not put on a footing more relevant to the twenty-first century.

Since the EU's proposal for the successor regime, with regional economic partnership agreements (REPAs) at its core, is not satisfactory, the task is to identify alternative strategies. These need to take account of the changes to be expected over the next five to ten years, the evidence of other relevant agreements and the varying needs of the different ACP States. The report approaches this task by:

❖ reviewing the trends in international trade policy that are undermining the effectiveness and credibility of the Lomé Convention;

❖ describing relevant examples of the type of agreement that the EU appears to have in mind in its REPA proposal;

❖ suggesting the broad lines of a strategy to implement the ACP's desire to extend the World Trade Organization (WTO) waiver on Lomé and to provide an adequate 'safety net' should subsequent negotiations prove to be unsatisfactory.

The Forces Undermining Lomé

The current negotiations are the most significant since those that gave birth to Lomé I. The WTO banana dispute has had a disproportionate impact by fracturing the shell of a relationship that had already been weakened by underlying change. The economic importance of the ACP to the EU is much less than it was in 1975; at the same time, the EU's trade policy relations with other, economically more important, regions have blossomed. So while Lomé I was unique in terms of the breadth, depth and institutional richness of its trade regime, Lomé IV is just one of many agreements and suffers from certain anomalies compared with more recent accords.

One of these anomalies is its status within the WTO framework. In its judgement on the EU banana regime the WTO Dispute Settlement Panel brought into question the compatibility of the entire Lomé relationship with international trade rules. Although the current waiver appears to have resolved the issue until February 2000, it will need to be replaced, when it expires, with a more robust justification. The reason for the use of the term 'appears' is that, as the dispute on bananas illustrated, the precise terms of a waiver can be subject to close scrutiny with the aim of striking down aspects of the regime that have not been supported unambiguously. It remains open, therefore, to WTO contracting parties to challenge parts of the Lomé relationship even before February 2000 if they believe that they cannot be supported by the precise wording of the waiver.

The WTO 'problem' is an intractable one since none of the 'pegs' that support discrimination in favour of certain developing countries but not others is entirely fool-proof. None of them provides a fully robust justification for the EU–ACP trade regime.

Even variations within the Generalised System of Preferences (GSP) could be subject to challenge. This was illustrated at the very end of the research project, when Brazil announced that it was lodging a complaint against the treatment by the EU of exports from the Andean Community of instant coffee. The special preferences for the Andean States are provided within the GSP – what has been called in this Report the 'Super' GSP.

Similarly, Article XXIV, which covers free trade areas and customs unions, might not provide defence against a challenge by an aggrieved State. The treatment accorded to the EU–South Africa free trade agreement (FTA), if it is concluded, may provide case law that would then apply to REPAs.

The WTO also presents a challenge to ACP preferences in a different sense. By presiding over further liberalisation of the products of particular interest under Lomé (clothing and temperate agriculture) it is contributing to the erosion of effective market access. Preference erosion has been a feature of EU–ACP trade policy for many years but, unless there is a sharp reversal in the trend of international trade policy formation, it is likely to accelerate markedly over the next five to ten years. The phasing out of the Multifibre Arrangement (MFA) will remove a major stimulus to clothing investment in ACP States and a key competitive advantage to ACP exports. The liberalisation of temperate agriculture may take longer to come into effect, but it would be imprudent for the ACP to assume that, for example, the Sugar and Beef Protocols will still offer them advantageous prices by the end of the next decade.

The loss of favourable prices for agricultural exports may come sooner. The EU's internal changes for the Common Agricultural Policy (CAP) may tend to focus on reforms that have a disproportionate adverse effect on the ACP. Moves, for example, to shift subsidies from con-sumers to tax-payers would result in price falls that would be offset for EU farmers (but not ACP suppliers) by direct transfers.

The Terms of a REPA

The EU has been vague about its plans for REPAs, but there exist examples from other agreements that provide guidance. A detailed analysis of the EU–Morocco Agreement suggests that there may be major pitfalls to be avoided by the ACP. The proposed terms of the EU–South Africa FTA reinforce this need for caution.

There is little reason to expect that ACP exports to the EU will derive significantly improved market access from a REPA. Both economic theory and the empirical evidence of the Morocco Agreement also suggest that the static and dynamic gains expected of liberalisation may occur only very partially. This is because opening up domestic markets to just one, not necessarily efficient, supplier in the absence of vigorous competition policy may not result in the expected changes in the structure of production.

The sections of the Morocco Agreement on 'new areas' of trade policy are particularly relevant to the ACP given that the EU has proposed that they should be introduced into the REPAs. These 'new areas' include policies on trade in services (including rights of establishment), competition policy and government procurement.

Of particular concern for the ACP should be the fact that, while Morocco is obliged to adopt EU competition rules, Europe has not forgone the right to use anti-dumping action. Given that the misuse of anti-dumping policy is widely considered to be one of the most disruptive features of the current international trade regime, and that the application of effective competition policy in the exporting State should remove the possibilities for predatory dumping, it is unfortunate that the FTA has not been used as a vehicle to introduce new disciplines. The ACP may wish to press for REPAs to include constraints upon the EU's use of anti-dumping policy. This is an area on which Lomé is silent and on which, therefore, a new agreement could represent an improvement.

Both the Morocco and the South Africa agreements suggest that the rules of origin in any REPA may be a problem for the ACP. The rules in the Lomé Convention are superior to those in both of these FTAs, in the sense that they are less of a constraint on ACP exports. Since the EU has indicated a desire to rationalise its multiplicity of origin rules, there is a danger that those incorporated into a REPA will differ from those in Lomé.

A Strategy

The ACP countries have indicated that they wish to obtain a WTO waiver to cover the period to 2010, and an integral part of the EU's proposal is that a waiver be sought which will last at least until 2005. Hence, any post-Lomé strategy is likely to incorporate some provision for obtaining a new WTO waiver.

The Report argues that:

❖ a carefully constructed waiver, accepted by consensus, would provide the ACP with legally secure preferences;

❖ this may be difficult to achieve.

It is very important that the ACP begin as soon as possible the task of building a consensus within the WTO in support of a waiver. It would be imprudent to rely on the EU to do this. Achieving such a consensus would require the overcoming of a range of possible objections from other developing countries and transition economies, as well as from some developed States.

As the banana panel ruling demonstrates, it is also vital that any waiver be drafted in such a way as to provide secure support for all those facets of the current trade regime that the ACP wish to pro-

tect. The required level of specificity will make the task of achieving a consensus more difficult because it will reduce the scope for compromise through the use of general terminology.

The ACP have indicated that the GSP as currently formulated represents an inadequate alternative to Lomé, but the possibility remains open that an improved one could form an important part of a post-Lomé strategy. At the very least, it would provide a safety net against the failure to obtain either a WTO waiver or acceptable terms for a REPA.

The Report identifies a strategy for improving the GSP in key areas. This would involve removing the deficiencies of the origin rules as compared with those in Lomé and providing a means whereby market access for non-least-developed ACP States could be brought up to Lomé standards.

No single criterion would distinguish all ACP States as a separate category. Such separation is required to allow the EU to offer to the ACP, and only to the ACP, improved terms under the GSP. Without it, the EU would have to generalise the improvements to a range of other medium-income and poor States. This would not only be politically unacceptable to the EU but would vitiate the objective of providing a competitive advantage to ACP States.

However, a combination of criteria can be devised which would tend to include all ACP States but exclude most others. It would involve a combination of income, vulnerability and size as the determinants of a group of States deserving of special treatment.

Identifying technical criteria is only the first stage; the key task would be to persuade other WTO members that this was a legitimate and acceptable method of classification. As in the case of a waiver, therefore, the main task for the ACP is the political challenge of pressing their case in the WTO. The function of technical reports such as this is to supply helpful analysis to support this political strategy.

Introduction to the Report

This report has been prepared to assist the ACP to develop a detailed strategy both for the current negotiations with the EU on a successor to the Lomé Convention, which will result in a broad 'Framework Agreement', and for the subsequent discussion on putting this into effect. Whilst the EU's proposed changes are unsatisfactory, it is also the case that the status quo is not an option since forces operating outside the Convention will undermine Lomé preferences if the relationship is not put on a footing more relevant to the twenty-first century.

For this reason, the formulation of an appropriate ACP strategy is neither a simple task nor one that is likely to be completed quickly. If it is to serve the ACP's economic and political needs into the next century, it must take account of the many changes in the world that have occurred since Lomé I was signed in 1975. The principal aim of this report is to assist in assessing the impact of these changes, the ways in which they require change to the EU–ACP relationship and the further changes that may be expected over the next five to ten years that will influence the environment within which the successor arrangement will operate.

The report is divided into three parts. Part 1 reviews the forces that are undermining the credibility of the Lomé Convention and which must be taken into account in the formulation of a successor regime. Given the EU's proposals for REPAs, Part 2 analyses two relevant examples: the free trade agreement negotiated between the EU and Morocco, and the agreement still under negotiation with South Africa. Part 3 sketches the broad lines of one possible strategy that would take account of the information conveyed in Parts 1 and 2.

Part 1

Costs and Benefits of Replacing Lomé

Introduction

The Lomé Convention used to sit at the centre of the EU's development policy as a unique agreement combining a liberal trade regime and substantial aid within a framework of jointly agreed principles and institutions. It is unique no longer: the EU now has a host of other preferential trade agreements, its aid to non-ACP States has been growing much faster and the Maastricht Treaty provides a broad statement of the aims of development co-operation. It is not just that relations with other States outside the Organisation for Economic Cooperation and Development (OECD) have been upgraded; to an extent, the ACP have been downgraded in terms of European interests.

The current ACP–EU negotiations are the most significant since those of the early 1970s that gave birth to Lomé I. This is because a chance set of events (the WTO banana dispute) has had a disproportionate impact by shattering the shell of a relationship that already had been fundamentally weakened by decades of gradual underlying change. The challenge is to negotiate a new relationship that responds to the realities of the new millennium. As explained below, neither a continuation of the status quo nor the EU's proposed changes adequately meet the challenge. To do so requires a broad understanding of the pressures that have undermined the old relationship.

Why Lomé is under pressure

Tensions between formal policy and effective interests

At the heart of this shift is an evolution of Europe's economic and political priorities.

A change in the structure of Europe's economy has led to a growing disparity between the focus of the EU's formal development policies and its economic and political interests in the South. At the same time, the collapse of communism to the East and concern with political and demographic patterns in its Southern neighbours have refocused political attention closer to home.

In recent decades there has been a change in the relative importance of various sources of European growth, with non-traded services and intra-developed country trade increasing in relative significance. The distortions caused by the CAP have simply accentuated a trend away from the traditional colonial trade pattern of importing raw materials from the South and exporting to it manufactures. In its place, a trade has developed with parts of the South that emphasises a two way flow of manufactures and services. But the ACP are not well represented in this new trade pattern.

The leaders in the new pattern of trade have been, on the European side, the States with relatively weak colonial ties (notably Germany) and, in the South, the countries of East and South East Asia. By contrast, formal development policy was fashioned in the 1970s and 1980s largely by the major ex-colonial States (France and the UK) and was focused on the recent colonies, particularly the ACP.

Over time a tension has developed between the focus of formal policy towards the South and the focus of the EU's immediate economic interests. The tension was initially defused because each EU Member State retained control over many of the most potent commercial policy instruments. Export credits, investment promotion and debt rescheduling remain Member State responsibilities; Germany, for example, may use them to promote its interests in South East Asia regardless of an EU focus on the ACP. Indeed, it might prefer the Union to concentrate on the ACP so as not to queer its pitch in Asia. But as powers are transferred increasingly from national to Union level this capacity to run an independent shadow policy withers; the emphasis of Union-level policy acquires a direct importance for national interests. This is the broader significance of the Single European Market (SEM) for EU–South relations.

The erosion of old policy instruments

Such changes come at a time when the foundations of the EU's relationship with the South are trembling. EU officials have managed over the years to fashion with some skill a quasi-foreign policy based on the limited range of Union-level instruments. Trade preferences bulk large in the relationship with the South. But the value of trade preferences to the beneficiary is related inversely to the level of protectionism (at least if the matter is viewed only in a short-term, static perspective). The 1990s have been a decade of liberalisation, reducing the value of any preferences.

Hence, the whole edifice built up over the years by the EU is subsiding gently as its foundations are weakened by liberalisation. Since this is happening at a time when the pace of European integration is fast (despite periodic reverses), a new edifice is likely to be thrown up to replace the old. The Union institutions will acquire a wider range of powers. Among them, no doubt, will be instruments that are of value to the South and may be used to construct a new relationship. But it does not follow that the new instruments will be used in support of the same objectives – or States – as the old. Arguably, for example, aid programmes (which are not a policy instrument for which a compelling argument can be made for Union competence) have been used as a quasi foreign policy tool in the absence of a proper EU foreign policy. If greater European integration results in a genuine Union-level foreign policy, justification for the aid 'substitute foreign policy' will disappear. That is the challenge for the ACP.

The impact of globalisation

The problems experienced with the WTO over Caribbean and African bananas have illustrated how difficult it is becoming to protect high-cost ACP producers from international competition. The banana problem is essentially a consequence of one example of globalisation: the creation of the SEM. By breaking down barriers with their EU partners, those European States that have traditionally supported high-priced imports from favoured developing countries are finding it difficult to continue. Similar problems are being experienced in clothing and other products where there were distinct national sub-markets before 1992.

Liberalisation will add to these problems. Lomé preferences will not lose all their vitality until the middle of the next decade because liberalisation will not reach all important products until then. But it is only a matter of time. The second most important Lomé preference is exemption from the MFA. Under the Uruguay Round the MFA will be phased out by the end of 2004.

This will leave just one really important Lomé preference: guaranteed prices under the Protocols for certain temperate agricultural products, and tariff cuts for many others. These are valuable to their ACP beneficiaries only as long as the CAP maintains artificially high prices in Europe. The CAP has withstood many attempts at fundamental reform, but it would be imprudent for the ACP to assume that it will not succumb during the next decade to the concurrent onslaughts of its costs to European consumers and taxpayers, the demands of EU enlargement to the East, and the next Round of WTO negotiations. The remaining five to ten year 'window of opportunity' must be grasped by as many ACP countries as possible. After it has closed they will face the harsh winds of global competition in all of their markets.

The EU's proposals

The EU has put forward a proposal to recast the relationship. This sub-section reviews it briefly. It does not go into great detail, since the objective of the report is to assist in the process of establishing an ACP proposal. All that is required in this context is evidence that the EU's proposal falls short of a totally satisfactory solution.

The EU proposal presents the ACP with a very stark choice: Lomé IV will expire in the year 2000, but its trade provisions will be continued only until 2005 to allow for the negotiation of a very different successor arrangement. The EU's preferred option is for all ACP sub-regions to negotiate REPAs, which can be justified internationally as FTAs and will certainly require some degree of reciprocity. Those non-least-developed (LDDC) ACP States that fail to join such agreements will be downgraded to the GSP. Any LDDC ACP States that are not in regional trade groups will be allowed to retain Lomé privileges if they do not join a REPA.

Downgrading to the GSP could be very costly to the ACP (see below). An analysis of the impact of imposing current GSP tariffs on current ACP exports to Europe shows that there would be a substantial financial transfer from the ACP to the EU treasury (Kennan and Stevens, 1997).

Another key feature of the proposal is that the period to 2000 should be used to negotiate a Framework Agreement of general principles with an indefinite duration. Since the Lomé Convention already contains a very full set of guiding principles, it must be assumed that the EU is seeking something different. But what? Since the framework will be of indefinite duration, it is very important that it provide an enabling, and not a constraining, framework.

Sources of uncertainty

The vagueness over the principles proposed for the Framework Agreement is only one of many areas of uncertainty in the EU's approach. Even technical calculations such as those on the cost of downgrading to the GSP can be only speculative because the scheme is likely to undergo change by 2005. The treatment of ACP States that do not sign REPAs is a little unclear. The least-developed have been promised a continuation of the same levels of market access. In the version of the mandate finally approved by the Member States in June 1998, the prospect was introduced that non-least-developed ACP countries outside a REPA might also be able to maintain their current access:

> Notwithstanding the primary objective set out in the mandate with regard to FTAs, the Council and the Commission agree to assess, in 2004, the situation of the non-LDC ACPs who are *for objective reasons* not in a position to join such FTAs with the EU (EU Council 1998: 18, footnote 1 [emphasis added]).

However, as the analysis in Part 3 shows, it may not be easy for the EU to deliver on this promise. It is important, therefore, for the ACP to be fully aware of the implication of a shift to current levels of GSP access.

Since it is clear that the proposals could have major implications, and so deserve the most serious attention by the ACP, it is reasonable that any strategy paper identify a set of questions that must be clarified at the outset. These include:

1. On what basis has the EU identified the regional sub-groups? The Framework Agreement should establish that the ACP alone can determine the membership of sub-groups (if there be any) with which the EU can negotiate.

2. What precisely is proposed for the commodity Protocols (including Sugar and Beef) under the post-Lomé arrangements? Since one of the stimuli for change is a perceived hostility towards

Lomé by some WTO members, it must be assumed that the continued existence of the Protocols is, at best, uncertain.

3. Would trade barriers need to be cut in relation to trade between members of the regional grouping, or only in relation to trade with the EU?

4. If the former, how much liberalisation would this require, and how practical a goal is it (given the very slow pace of regional liberalisation in the past)?

5. If the latter, what measures would be required (and how practical are they) to prevent trade diversion (e.g. Zimbabwe evading barriers on direct exports to Tanzania by routing them via the EU)?

6. Given that the EU–South Africa FTA negotiations have taken three years and are still incomplete, how realistic is it to expect the more extensive negotiations with a much larger number of administrations to be completed within the proposed transition period (apparently five years)? How is DGVIII to be reorganised to cope with such wide-ranging negotiations?

The cost of transfer to the GSP

If in 2005 the EU transferred to the Standard GSP all non-least-developed ACP States, how serious would this be? The current GSP is described below (in the section on 'The Stimulus for Trade Liberalisation'). Unless it is extended and deepened during the intervening period, it will result in an increase in the EU's applied tariffs for a range of ACP exports. This is undesirable from the viewpoints both of development and of a liberal European trade policy. The products and countries that would be affected have been identified in a study completed in 1997 by Jane Kennan and Christopher Stevens using 1995 data. The findings are summarised below and are

taken up again in Part 3, where possible variations on the current GSP are considered.

Types of effect

The *status quo* is that a substantial number of ACP States enjoy useful preferences on products for which their main competitors are middle-income or richer countries. If Lomé access were to be replaced for non-least-developed ACP States by the standard GSP, these preference margins would be vulnerable. In principle there could be four possible changes in the ACP's relative terms of access (which might be combined for a given product, depending upon the current access of competitors). These are, in ascending order of European illiberalism:

❖ a preference might be retained, but on a reduced scale (in cases where some competitors trade on most favoured nation (MFN) terms and a GSP preference exists), e.g. Zimbabwe and Senegal would face reduced preferences over the USA for tobacco and groundnut oil respectively;

❖ a preference might be extinguished (where a competitor also trades on standard GSP terms or, if no GSP is available, on MFN terms), e.g. the Lomé Beef Protocol beneficiaries would lose their advantage over Mercosur (Mercado Común del Sur) exporters;

❖ a situation of equality could be replaced by one of discrimination (where the terms under Lomé are the same as those available to a competitor, but the GSP rate is less favourable), e.g. the 11 ACP exporters of beans would face discrimination in favour of, generally richer, Mediterranean States;

❖ a preference could be replaced by discrimination (where Lomé accords the ACP more favourable access than is available to its competitors, but the GSP would provide less favourable access). There is just one case of this: Ecuador would enjoy advantages over ACP frozen shrimp exporters.

The countries and products affected

The products and ACP States that would be affected in these ways are identified in Table 1. This is divided into sections based on the foregoing categories, and identifies for each the product, the ACP exporters and the major competitors concerned. Unless the Standard GSP for each of the products identified in the table is improved to the current Lomé level, the ACP States listed will experience a deterioration in their terms of access to the EU market if they fail to conclude economic partnership agreements.

They will be negotiating such agreements, therefore, under duress.

Despite the widespread view that Lomé preferences have not been well utilised, Table 1 indicates that *every single* non-least-developed ACP State would face a relative deterioration of access if the GSP is not improved. In the great majority of cases, the main 'beneficiary' of this change would be an upper-middle-income or rich State.[1] The States that would be affected on the largest number of products are Côte d'Ivoire and Nigeria (on 21 and 20 products respectively). A further nine States (Ghana, Zimbabwe, Mauritius, Senegal, Jamaica, Cameroon, Kenya, Dominican Republic, and Trinidad and Tobago) would be affected on ten or more products.

Table 1. Products on which the ACP may lose preferences

CN 1995	Description (abbreviated)	Non-LDDC ACP exporters	Competitor(s)[a]
Preference reduced			
03061390	frozen shrimps and prawns (excl. 'pandalidae' and 'crangon')	Nigeria, Senegal, Surinam, Gabon, C.d'Ivoire, Congo, Cameroon, Kenya, Trinidad & Tobago, Ghana, Guyana	Thailand
08043000	fresh or dried pineapples	C.d'Ivoire, Ghana, Dominican Rep., Cameroon, Mauritius, Swaziland, Kenya, Zimbabwe, Nigeria, Senegal	Thailand
15081090	crude ground-nut oil (excl. for industrial uses)	Senegal, Nigeria	USA
15111090	crude palm oil (excl. for industrial uses)	PNG, C.d'Ivoire, Ghana, Gabon, Cameroon, Nigeria, Senegal	Indonesia, Malaysia
18031000	cocoa paste (excl. defatted)	C.d'Ivoire, Cameroon, Ghana, Nigeria, Dominican Rep.	Brazil
18040000	cocoa butter, fat and oil	Ghana, C.d'Ivoire, Nigeria, Cameroon, Dominican Rep.	Brazil
21011011	solid extracts, essences and concentrates of coffee	C.d'Ivoire, Ghana, Nigeria, Senegal	Brazil
24012010	partly or wholly stemmed or stripped flue-cured Virginia type tobacco	Zimbabwe, Ghana, Kenya, Barbados, Nigeria, Trinidad & Tobago	USA, Brazil
61051000	men's or boys' shirts of cotton, knitted or crocheted	Mauritius, Dominican Rep., Zimbabwe, Nigeria, Jamaica	Hong Kong, China

1   Bearing in mind that the analysis only covers the three most important competitive suppliers.

CN 1995	Description (abbreviated)	Non-LDDC ACP exporters	Competitor(s)[a]
61101031	men's or boys' jerseys and similar articles, of wool, knitted or crocheted	Mauritius, Jamaica, Zimbabwe	Hong Kong
61101091	women's or girls' jerseys and similar articles, of wool, knitted or crocheted	Mauritius, Jamaica, Ghana, Dominican Rep., Namibia	Hong Kong, China, Macao
61102099	women's or girls' jerseys and similar articles, of cotton, knitted or crocheted	Mauritius, Jamaica, Dominican Rep., Zimbabwe, C.d'Ivoire, Fiji, Nigeria, Senegal, Kenya, Barbados	Hong Kong, China
62052000	men's or boys' shirts of cotton	Mauritius, Kenya, Zimbabwe, Fiji, Jamaica, Dominican Rep., C.d'Ivoire, Barbados, Senegal, St Kitts & Nevis, Dominica, Nigeria, Ghana, Surinam, Bahamas, Trinidad & Tobago	Hong Kong
72024199	ferro-chromium, containing by weight > 6% carbon and > 60% chromium	Zimbabwe	Russia

Preference extinguished

02013000	fresh or chilled bovine meat, boneless	Zimbabwe, Namibia, Swaziland, Guyana, Antigua & Barbuda	Argentina, Brazil, Uruguay
03026996	saltwater fish, edible, fresh or chilled, n.e.s.	Senegal, C.d'Ivoire, Trinidad & Tobago, Belize, Seychelles, Ghana, Jamaica, Nigeria, Kenya, Namibia, PNG, Mauritius, Grenada, Zimbabwe	Croatia
03037810	frozen hake 'merluccius spp.'	Namibia	Argentina, Chile, S.Africa
03042057	frozen fillets of hake 'merluccius'	Namibia, Senegal, St Vincent, Antigua & Barbuda	Argentina, Peru, Chile
03061390	frozen shrimps and prawns (excl. 'pandalidae' and 'crangon')	Nigeria, Senegal, Surinam, Gabon, C.d'Ivoire, Congo, Cameroon, Kenya, Trinidad & Tobago, Ghana, Guyana	India
06031069	fresh cut flowers and buds from 1 November to 31 May	Kenya, Zimbabwe, C.d'Ivoire, Mauritius, Surinam, Jamaica, Namibia, Cameroon, Swaziland, Barbados, St Vincent, Trinidad & Tobago, Grenada, Nigeria, Guyana, Dominican Rep.	S.Africa
08030019	bananas, fresh (excl. plantains)	C.d'Ivoire, Cameroon, St Lucia, Jamaica, St Vincent, Belize, Surinam, Dominica, Grenada	Ecuador, Costa Rica, Colombia
08043000	fresh or dried pineapples	C.d'Ivoire, Ghana, Dominican Rep., Cameroon, Mauritius, Swaziland, Kenya, Zimbabwe, Nigeria, Senegal	S.Africa, Brazil
15081090	crude ground-nut oil (excl. for industrial uses)	Senegal, Nigeria	Argentina, Brazil
15111090	crude palm oil (excl. for industrial uses)	PNG, C.d'Ivoire, Ghana, Gabon, Cameroon, Nigeria, Senegal	Brazil
16041414	tunas and skipjack, prepared or preserved in vegetable oil	C.d'Ivoire, Mauritius, Ghana, Senegal, Fiji, Seychelles, Namibia	Thailand, Philippines

CN 1995	Description (abbreviated)	Non-LDDC ACP exporters	Competitor(s)[a]
16041418	tunas and skipjack, prepared or preserved	C.d'Ivoire, Senegal, Mauritius, Ghana, Seychelles, Fiji, Namibia	Thailand, Philippines
17011110	raw cane sugar, for refining	Mauritius, Fiji, Guyana, Swaziland, Jamaica, Zimbabwe, Trinidad & Tobago, Belize, Barbados, St Kitts & Nevis, Congo	Brazil, Cuba
17011190	raw cane sugar (excl. for refining)	Mauritius, Barbados, Swaziland, Zimbabwe	Brazil, Cuba S.Africa
18031000	cocoa paste (excl. defatted)	C.d'Ivoire, Cameroon, Ghana, Nigeria, Dominican Rep.	Indonesia
18040000	cocoa butter, fat and oil	Ghana, C.d'Ivoire, Nigeria, Cameroon, Dominican Rep.	Malaysia, Indonesia
22084090	rum and taffia, in containers holding > 2 l	Trinidad & Tobago, Bahamas, Guyana, Jamaica, Barbados, St Lucia, C.d'Ivoire	Cuba, Brazil
24012010	partly or wholly stemmed or stripped flue-cured Virginia type tobacco	Zimbabwe, Ghana, Kenya, Barbados, Nigeria, Trinidad & Tobago	Argentina
28182000	aluminium oxide	Jamaica, Surinam	USA, Australia
29051100	methanol 'methyl alcohol'	Trinidad & Tobago, Bahamas	Libya, Russia
41051210	unsplit sheep or lamb skin leather, pre-tanned	Nigeria, Kenya, Cameroon	Saudi Arabia, Brazil
41061200	goat or kidskin leather, dehaired, mineral/synthetic pre-tanned only	Nigeria, Kenya, Cameroon, C.d'Ivoire, Dominican Rep.	Nepal, Pakistan, China
61091000	t-shirts, singlets and other vests of cotton, knitted or crocheted	Mauritius, Kenya, Zimbabwe, C.d'Ivoire, Fiji, Nigeria, Dominican Rep., Jamaica, Senegal, Bahamas, Trinidad & Tobago	India
62052000	men's or boys' shirts of cotton	Mauritius, Kenya, Zimbabwe, Fiji, Jamaica, Dominican Rep., C.d'Ivoire, Barbados, Senegal, St Kitts & Nevis, Dominica, Nigeria, Ghana, Surinam, Bahamas, Trinidad & Tobago	India
76011000	aluminium, not alloyed, unwrought	Ghana, Cameroon, Surinam, C.d'Ivoire, Namibia, Guyana	Russia, Canada

Equality replaced by discrimination

03026996	saltwater fish, edible, fresh or chilled, n.e.s	Senegal, C.d'Ivoire, Trinidad & Tobago, Belize, Seychelles, Ghana, Jamaica, Nigeria, Kenya, Namibia, PNG, Mauritius, Grenada, Zimbabwe	Morocco, Turkey
06031051	fresh cut roses and buds from 1 November to 31 May	Kenya, Zimbabwe, Swaziland, Nigeria, Mauritius, Senegal, C.d'Ivoire	Israel, Ecuador, Colombia
06031069	fresh cut flowers and buds from 1 November to 31 May	Kenya, Zimbabwe, C.d'Ivoire, Mauritius, Surinam, Jamaica, Namibia, Cameroon, Swaziland, Barbados, St Vincent, Trinidad & Tobago, Grenada, Nigeria, Guyana, Dominican Rep.	Israel, Ecuador
07082010	fresh or chilled beans 'vigna spp., phaseolus spp.' from 1 October	Kenya, Senegal, Zimbabwe, Cameroon, Dominican Rep., Surinam, Nigeria,	Egypt, Morocco, Turkey

CN 1995	Description (abbreviated)	Non-LDDC ACP exporters	Competitor(s)[a]
	to 30 June	Swaziland, C.d'Ivoire, St Lucia, Ghana	
16041414	tunas and skipjack, prepared or preserved in vegetable oil	C.d'Ivoire, Mauritius, Ghana, Senegal, Fiji, Seychelles, Namibia	Turkey
16041418	tunas and skipjack, prepared or preserved	C.d'Ivoire, Senegal, Mauritius, Ghana, Seychelles, Fiji, Namibia	Colombia
18031000	cocoa paste (excl. defatted)	C.d'Ivoire, Cameroon, Ghana, Nigeria, Dominican Rep.	Norway
21011011	solid extracts, essences and concentrates of coffee	C.d'Ivoire, Ghana, Nigeria, Senegal	Colombia, Switz.
22084090	rum and taffia, in containers l holding > 2	Trinidad & Tobago, Bahamas, Guyana, Jamaica, Barbados, St Lucia, C.d'Ivoire	Cyprus
28182000	aluminium oxide	Jamaica, Surinam	Hungary
29051100	methanol 'methyl alcohol'	Trinidad & Tobago, Bahamas	Venezuela
41051210	unsplit sheep or lamb skin leather, pre-tanned	Nigeria, Kenya, Cameroon	Algeria
61051000	men's or boys' shirts of cotton, knitted or crocheted	Mauritius, Dominican Rep., Zimbabwe, Nigeria, Jamaica	Turkey
61091000	t-shirts, singlets and other vests of cotton, knitted or crocheted	Mauritius, Kenya, Zimbabwe, C.d'Ivoire, Fiji, Nigeria, Dominican Rep., Jamaica, Senegal, Bahamas, Trinidad & Tobago	Turkey, Bangladesh
61101031	men's or boys' jerseys and similar articles, of wool, knitted or crocheted	Mauritius, Jamaica, Zimbabwe	Tunisia, Croatia
61102099	women's or girls' jerseys and similar articles, of cotton, knitted or crocheted	Mauritius, Jamaica, Dominican Rep., Zimbabwe, C.d'Ivoire, Fiji, Nigeria, Senegal, Kenya, Barbados	Turkey
62052000	men's or boys' shirts of cotton	Mauritius, Kenya, Zimbabwe, Fiji, Jamaica, Dominican Rep., C.d'Ivoire, Barbados, Senegal, St Kitts & Nevis, Dominica, Nigeria, Ghana, Surinam, Bahamas, Trinidad & Tobago	Bangladesh
72024199	ferro-chromium, containing by weight > 6% carbon and > 60% chromium	Zimbabwe	Norway, Latvia
76011000	aluminium, not alloyed, unwrought	Ghana, Cameroon, Surinam, C.d'Ivoire, Namibia, Guyana	Norway

Preference replaced by discrimination

CN 1995	Description (abbreviated)	Non-LDDC ACP exporters	Competitor(s)[a]
03061390	frozen shrimps and prawns (excl. 'pandalidae' and 'crangon')	Nigeria, Senegal, Surinam, Gabon, C.d'Ivoire, Congo, Cameroon, Kenya, Trinidad & Tobago, Ghana, Guyana	Ecuador

No change

CN 1995	Description (abbreviated)	Non-LDDC ACP exporters	Competitor(s)[a]
08030019	bananas, fresh (excl. plantains)	Dominican Rep., Ghana, Kenya, Gabon, Bahamas	Ecuador, Costa Rica, Colombia

Note: (a) The three largest non-LDDC ACP competitors.
Sources: Eurostat 1996; GSP 1994 and 1996; Taric 1996.

The largest category, in terms of the number of products affected and the number of ACP country references, is that of 'preference extinguished'. But a close second is the 'equality replaced by discrimination' group.

The scale of the potential loss

If imports from ACP States currently enter the EU duty free but henceforth will pay a tariff, there will necessarily be a transfer of income from elements in the ACP supply chain to the European treasury. Without knowing a great deal about the details of the supply chain (how much of the final price goes to supermarkets, to importers, to shippers, to exporters, to producers, etc.) it is not possible to determine how this transfer will affect demand. But, in order to retain the same post-customs price relationship between imports from the ACP and from other sources, the revenue to be distributed among elements of the supply chain has to be reduced by the size of the import tax. The European treasury's gain, therefore, is the ACP supply chain's loss.

In order to give an indication of the potential scale of this change, an exercise was undertaken that applied to the value/volume of 1995 imports the difference in tariff between Lomé rates and those obtained by linking the Standard GSP to the post-Uruguay Round MFN. The results of this analysis are presented in Table 2.[2]

Table 2. ACP preference loss: the potential forex costs

CN 1995 and description	Non-LDDC ACP exporters	Exports to EU 1995 Ecu'000	Tons	Tariff increase	Monetary equivalent Ecu'000	% of total monetary equivalent
Most valuable ACP group exports (Group 1)						
03061390 frozen shrimps and prawns (excl. 'pandalidae' and 'crangon')					3,405	0.4%
	Nigeria	33,091		4.2%	1,390	
	Senegal	26,446		4.2%	1,111	
	Surinam	6,611		4.2%	278	
	Gabon	5,882		4.2%	247	
	C.d'Ivoire	3,659		4.2%	154	
	Congo	1,934		4.2%	81	
	Cameroon	1,787		4.2%	75	
	Kenya	1,335		4.2%	56	
	Trinidad & Tobago	159		4.2%	7	
	Ghana	131		4.2%	6	
	Guyana	48		4.2%	2	
08030019 bananas, fresh (excl. plantains)					47,882	6.2%
	C.d'Ivoire	85,011	160,268	75 Ecu/T	12,020	
	Cameroon	79,589	138,318	75 Ecu/T	10,374	
	St Lucia	54,609	101,492	75 Ecu/T	7,612	
	Jamaica	49,663	83,751	75 Ecu/T	6,281	
	St Vincent	26,008	47,673	75 Ecu/T	3,575	
	Belize	23,714	41,126	75 Ecu/T	3,084	
	Dominica	18,343	33,260	75 Ecu/T	2,495	
	Surinam	18,572	27,984	75 Ecu/T	2,099	
	Grenada	2,398	4,558	75 Ecu/T	342	

2   Certain small and anomalous exports have been excluded, such as beef exports from Antigua and Guyana, which are not Beef Protocol beneficiaries, sugar exports from Nigeria, and products such as rum which have such complex tariffs that specialist knowledge is required.

CN 1995 and description	Non-LDDC ACP exporters	Exports to EU 1995		Tariff increase	Monetary equivalent Ecu'000	% of total monetary equivalent
		Ecu'000	Tons			
15111090	crude palm oil (excl. for industrial uses)				1,474	0.2%
	PNG	89,987		1.3%	1,170	
	C.d'Ivoire	18,912		1.3%	246	
	Ghana	2,233		1.3%	29	
	Gabon	1,211		1.3%	16	
	Cameroon	1,006		1.3%	13	
	Nigeria	31		1.3%	0	
	Senegal	4		1.3%	0	
16041418	tunas and skipjack, prepared or preserved				48,040	6.3%
	C.d'Ivoire	128,964		24.0%	30,951	
	Senegal	28,578		24.0%	6,859	
	Mauritius	15,031		24.0%	3,607	
	Ghana	12,265		24.0%	2,944	
	Seychelles	7,539		24.0%	1,809	
	Fiji	5,401		24.0%	1,296	
	Namibia	2,390		24.0%	574	
17011110	raw cane sugar, for refining				469,433	61.2%
	Mauritius	239,981	456,411	339 Ecu/T	154,723	
	Swaziland	86,282	180,902	339 Ecu/T	61,326	
	Fiji	93,227	179,402	339 Ecu/T	60,817	
	Guyana	89,602	174,390	339 Ecu/T	59,118	
	Jamaica	73,980	141,326	339 Ecu/T	47,910	
	Zimbabwe	29,898	67,519	339 Ecu/T	22,889	
	Trinidad & Tobago	29,719	58,666	339 Ecu/T	19,888	
	Belize	28,109	55,228	339 Ecu/T	18,722	
	Barbados	17,577	33,423	339 Ecu/T	11,330	
	St Kitts & Nevis	10,340	19,579	339 Ecu/T	6,637	
	Congo	9,523	17,911	339 Ecu/T	6,072	
18040000	cocoa butter, fat and oil				6,571	0.9%
	Ghana	52,152		5.4%	2,816	
	C.d'Ivoire	46,750		5.4%	2,525	
	Nigeria	13,170		5.4%	711	
	Cameroon	9,373		5.4%	506	
	Dominican Rep.	244		5.4%	13	
24012010	partly or wholly stemmed or stripped flue-cured Virginia type tobacco				16,281	2.1%
	Zimbabwe	103,205		15.6%	16,100	
	Ghana	341		15.6%	53	
	Kenya	321		15.6%	50	
	Barbados	288		15.6%	45	
	Nigeria	209		15.6%	33	
	Trinidad & Tobago	1		15.6%	0	
28182000	aluminium oxide				8,636	1.1%
	Jamaica	168,493		4.0%	6,740	
	Surinam	47,413		4.0%	1,897	

CN 1995 and description	Non-LDDC ACP exporters	Exports to EU 1995 Ecu'000	Tons	Tariff increase	Monetary equivalent Ecu'000	% of total monetary equivalent
61091000 t-shirts, singlets and other vests of cotton, knitted or crocheted					10,075	1.3%
	Mauritius	93,174		10.2%	9,504	
	Kenya	1,528		10.2%	156	
	Zimbabwe	1,110		10.2%	113	
	C.d'Ivoire	891		10.2%	91	
	Fiji	860		10.2%	88	
	Nigeria	677		10.2%	69	
	Dominican Rep.	370		10.2%	38	
	Jamaica	142		10.2%	14	
	Senegal	13		10.2%	1	
	Bahamas	8		10.2%	1	
	Trinidad & Tobago	3		10.2%	0	
	Barbados	1		10.2%	0	
76011000 aluminium, not alloyed, unwrought					18,853	2.5%
	Ghana	170,856		6.0%	10,251	
	Cameroon	92,426		6.0%	5,546	
	Surinam	50,702		6.0%	3,042	
	C.d'Ivoire	104		6.0%	6	
	Namibia	88		6.0%	5	
	Guyana	41		6.0%	2	

Most important individual non-LDDC country exports (Group 2)

CN 1995 and description	Non-LDDC ACP exporters	Exports to EU 1995 Ecu'000	Tons	Tariff increase	Monetary equivalent Ecu'000	% of total monetary equivalent
02013000 fresh or chilled bovine meat, boneless					37,697	4.9%
	Zimbabwe	30,681	6,156	12.8%+2589 Ecu/T	19,865	
	Namibia	22,775	5,546	12.8%+2589 Ecu/T	17,274	
	Swaziland	720	180	12.8%+2589 Ecu/T	558	
03026996 saltwater fish, edible, fresh or chilled, n.e.s.					1,657	0.2%
	Senegal	29,442		5.3%	1,560	
	C.d'Ivoire	918		5.3%	49	
	Trinidad & Tobago	255		5.3%	14	
	Belize	206		5.3%	11	
	Seychelles	206		5.3%	11	
	Ghana	127		5.3%	7	
	Jamaica	60		5.3%	3	
	Nigeria	10		5.3%	1	
	Kenya	9		5.3%	0	
	Namibia	9		5.3%	0	
	PNG	9		5.3%	0	
	Mauritius	3		5.3%	0	
	Grenada	3		5.3%	0	
	Zimbabwe	1		5.3%	0	
03037810 frozen hake 'merluccius spp.'					5,943	0.8%
	Namibia	39,617		15.0%	5,943	
03042057 frozen fillets of hake 'merluccius'					2,929	0.4%
	Namibia	45,676		6.4%	2,923	
	Senegal	44		6.4%	3	
	St Vincent	40		6.4%	3	
	Antigua & Barbuda	10		6.4%	1	

CN 1995 and description	Non-LDDC ACP exporters	Exports to EU 1995 Ecu'000	Tons	Tariff increase	Monetary equivalent Ecu'000	% of total monetary equivalent
06031051 fresh cut roses and buds from 1 November to 31 May					3,428	0.4%
	Kenya	21,250		8.5%	1,806	
	Zimbabwe	18,714		8.5%	1,591	
	Swaziland	256		8.5%	22	
	Nigeria	98		8.5%	8	
	Mauritius	6		8.5%	1	
	Senegal	3		8.5%	0	
	C.d'Ivoire	1		8.5%	0	
06031069 fresh cut flowers and buds from 1 November to 31 May					2,816	0.4%
	Kenya	20,083		8.5%	1,707	
	Zimbabwe	10,486		8.5%	891	
	C.d'Ivoire	1,067		8.5%	91	
	Mauritius	972		8.5%	83	
	Surinam	152		8.5%	13	
	Jamaica	109		8.5%	9	
	Namibia	70		8.5%	6	
	Cameroon	49		8.5%	4	
	Swaziland	38		8.5%	3	
	Barbados	35		8.5%	3	
	St Vincent	27		8.5%	2	
	Trinidad & Tobago	21		8.5%	2	
	Grenada	8		8.5%	1	
	Nigeria	6		8.5%	1	
	Guyana	5		8.5%	0	
	Dominican Rep.	5		8.5%	0	
07082010 fresh or chilled beans 'vigna spp., phaseolus spp.' from 1 October to 30 June					3,059	0.4%
	Kenya	25,305		8.8%	2,227	
	Senegal	4,612		8.8%	406	
	Zimbabwe	2,051		8.8%	180	
	Cameroon	2,023		8.8%	178	
	Dominican Rep.	456		8.8%	40	
	Surinam	288		8.8%	25	
	Nigeria	15		8.8%	1	
	Swaziland	5		8.8%	0	
	C.d'Ivoire	4		8.8%	0	
	St Lucia	4		8.8%	0	
	Ghana	3		8.8%	0	
08043000 fresh or dried pineapples					4,040	0.5%
	C.d'Ivoire	71,283		4.9%	3,493	
	Ghana	7,621		4.9%	373	
	Dominican Rep.	1,804		4.9%	88	
	Cameroon	1,184		4.9%	58	
	Mauritius	388		4.9%	19	
	Swaziland	77		4.9%	4	
	Kenya	60		4.9%	3	
	Zimbabwe	17		4.9%	1	
	Nigeria	10		4.9%	0	
	Senegal	2		4.9%	0	

CN 1995 and description	Non-LDDC ACP exporters	Exports to EU 1995 Ecu'000	Tons	Tariff increase	Monetary equivalent Ecu'000	% of total monetary equivalent
15081090 crude ground-nut oil (excl. for industrial uses)					3,064	0.4%
	Senegal	64,502		4.5%	2,903	
	Nigeria	3,595		4.5%	162	
16041414 tunas and skipjack, prepared or preserved, whole or in pieces, in vegetable oil					16,301	2.1%
	C.d'Ivoire	30,447		24.0%	7,307	
	Mauritius	9,835		24.0%	2,360	
	Ghana	8,795		24.0%	2,111	
	Senegal	7,988		24.0%	1,917	
	Fiji	5,424		24.0%	1,302	
	Seychelles	4,969		24.0%	1,193	
	Namibia	462		24.0%	111	
17011190 raw cane sugar (excl. for refining)					24,290	3.2%
	Mauritius	35,616	51,805	419 Ecu/T	21,706	
	Barbados	2,158	3,161	419 Ecu/T	1,324	
	Swaziland	994	1,760	419 Ecu/T	737	
	Zimbabwe	329	1,245	419 Ecu/T	522	
18031000 cocoa paste (excl. defatted)					2,228	0.3%
	C.d'Ivoire	25,225		6.7%	1,690	
	Cameroon	4,561		6.7%	306	
	Ghana	2,859		6.7%	192	
	Nigeria	529		6.7%	35	
	Dominican Rep.	80		6.7%	5	
21011011 solid extracts, essences and concentrates of coffee					1,599	0.2%
	C.d'Ivoire	49,501		3.2%	1,584	
	Ghana	317		3.2%	10	
	Nigeria	146		3.2%	5	
	Senegal	15		3.2%	0	
29051100 methanol 'methyl alcohol'					3,562	0.5%
	Trinidad & Tobago	90,375		3.9%	3,525	
	Bahamas	959		3.9%	37	
41051210 unsplit sheep or lamb skin leather, pre-tanned					659	0.1%
	Nigeria	31,608		2.0%	632	
	Kenya	758		2.0%	15	
	Cameroon	595		2.0%	12	
41061200 goat or kidskin leather, dehaired, mineral/synthetic pre-tanned only					980	0.1%
	Nigeria	41,041		2.0%	821	
	Kenya	7,287		2.0%	146	
	Cameroon	452		2.0%	9	
	C.d'Ivoire	145		2.0%	3	
	Dominican Rep.	74		2.0%	1	
61051000 men's or boys' shirts of cotton, knitted or crocheted					3,594	0.5%
	Mauritius	33,751		10.2%	3,443	
	Dominican Rep.	1,299		10.2%	132	

CN 1995 and description	Non-LDDC ACP exporters	Exports to EU 1995 Ecu'000	Tons	Tariff increase	Monetary equivalent Ecu'000	% of total monetary equivalent
	Zimbabwe	96		10.2%	10	
	Nigeria	58		10.2%	6	
	Jamaica	32		10.2%	3	
61101031 men's or boys' jerseys and similar articles, of wool, knitted or crocheted					3,751	0.5%
	Mauritius	32,316		10.2%	3,296	
	Jamaica	4,457		10.2%	455	
	Zimbabwe	3		10.2%	0	
61101091 men's or girls' jerseys and similar articles, of wool, knitted or crocheted					4,760	0.6%
	Mauritius	40,418		10.2%	4,123	
	Jamaica	5,506		10.2%	562	
	Ghana	719		10.2%	73	
	Dominican Rep.	24		10.2%2		
	Namibia	2		10.2%	0	
61102099 men's or girls' jerseys and similar articles, of cotton, knitted or crocheted					3,906	0.5%
	Mauritius	26,705		10.2%	2,724	
	Jamaica	9,204		10.2%	939	
	Dominican Rep.	1,192		10.2%	122	
	Zimbabwe	829		10.2%	85	
	C.d'Ivoire	168		10.2%	17	
	Fiji	117		10.2%	12	
	Nigeria	66		10.2%	7	
	Senegal	7		10.2%	1	
	Kenya	2		10.2%	0	
	Barbados	1		10.2%	0	
62052000 men's or boys' shirts of cotton					4,173	0.5%
	Mauritius	38,245		10.2%	3,901	
	Kenya	1,177		10.2%	120	
	Zimbabwe	661		10.2%	67	
	Fiji	459		10.2%	47	
	Jamaica	207		10.2%	21	
	Dominican Rep.	61		10.2%	6	
	C.d'Ivoire	22		10.2%	2	
	Barbados	20		10.2%	2	
	Senegal	17		10.2%	2	
	St Kitts & Nevis	14		10.2%	1	
	Dominica	7		10.2%	1	
	Nigeria	6		10.2%	1	
	Ghana	6		10.2%	1	
	Surinam	5		10.2%	1	
	Bahamas	2		10.2%	0	
	Trinidad & Tobago	1		10.2%	0	
72024199 ferro-chromium, containing by weight > 6% carbon and > 60% chromium					1,924	0.3%
	Zimbabwe	56,578		3.4%	1,924	
Total monetary equivalent					767,012	100.0%

Sources: Eurostat 1996; GSP 1994 and 1996; WTO 1996.

The total 'foreign exchange forgone' is in the region of Ecu 767 million per year. Overwhelmingly the most important foreign exchange loss would occur in relation to sugar (almost two-thirds of the total). Tuna and bananas, followed by beef, would be the next most affected. A further 19 products would incur foreign exchange losses of over Ecu 2.5 million a year.

The way forward

It is clear from the preceding section that there is a need for change: a continuation of the *status quo* is not an option since, even if there were to be a Lomé V identical in all respects to Lomé IV, the forces operating outside the Convention would continue to erode the benefits that the ACP obtain. But it is also clear that the EU's proposals are sufficiently flawed to make desirable the preparation of alternatives that are ACP-designed and put ACP needs at centre stage. But these proposals must take account of the pressures being exerted by the various stimuli for change. Otherwise they risk being overtaken by events. The remainder of Part 1 examines four sets of stimuli for change:

❖ pressure in the WTO;

❖ liberalisation (preferential and multilateral);

❖ reform of the CAP;

❖ EU enlargement and deeper integration.

In each case, it identifies the reasons why change is affecting the EU–ACP relationship, what may happen in future and the implications for the ACP.

The Stimulus of WTO Rules

The origin of problems with the WTO: bananas

When the Lomé Convention was signed it stood apart from the Community's other trade relations in terms of the breadth and boldness of its vision. Now it is just one of the EU's trade agreements that provide some States with access to the European market that is more liberal than that available under MFN treatment. All have evolved over the years and in an international environment that differs markedly from that of today. There is now serious concern that they are incompatible with WTO rules.

To a certain extent the rules administered by the WTO are more stringent than the old regime under the General Agreement on Tariffs and Trade (GATT), but this is not the main source of change. Rather, it is a change of attitudes: exceptions from MFN treatment are now viewed in a more sceptical light than in times past. In the opinion of the EU, the preferential access provided to ACP exports was justified under Article XXIV of the GATT read in the light of Part IV and, in particular, Article XXXVI para. 8 under which developed countries 'do not expect reciprocity' for preferences given in trade negotiations to less developed countries.

This position was challenged in 1993 by the GATT panel established to investigate Latin American complaints concerning the European banana regime. Since the aftershocks of this challenge are still being felt, and their implications for the EU's non-multilateral system is uncertain, it is important to be clear precisely what the banana dispute was about.

Origins

The problem arose from the difficulty of balancing three sets of demands:

❖ those arising from the changes required of balancing three sets of demands;

❖ the EU's treaty obligations under the Lomé Convention;

❖ the EU's obligations under the GATT.

Whilst often protrayed in terms of a simple clash between 'liberal traders versus protectionists', the range of interests underlying the conflicting positions was more complex. The completion of the SEM involved changes to the market for bananas because they were one of the few agricultural products not yet covered by common rules. Not only were bananas not subject to the CAP, they were also not subject, in effect, to the Common Commercial Policy. As a result there were three tariff regimes operating within Europe: duty-free imports by virtue of preferences for specific exporters under the Lom_ Convention's Banana Protocol (in France, UK and Italy); duty-free imports by virtue of a special derogation for the importer (Germany); and 20 per cent duty-paid imports in the B enelux countries, Ireland and Denmark.

Relatively high-priced Caribbean and African bananas found a market in the first group of States. Lower-priced 'dollar' fruit from Latin America dominated in the other two.

This differentiated regime survived because Member States could use licensing to control direct imports of 'non-preferred' fruit and Article 115 to control indirect imports. Both mechanisms fell victim to the SEM. They had either to be replaced by something else or the preferred suppliers would lose market share to the lower-cost dollar fruit.

The new regime

The solution adopted by the EU was to implement a two-tier import regime. A temporary regime was introduced to cover the first half of 1993, and a permanent system established thereafter. In both cases Caribbean and African bananas continue to enter the Union duty free, but dollar fruit are subject to a two-tier tariff. A tariff quota (set initially at two million tonnes) of imports from Latin America pay a specific duty of Ecu 100 per tonne (equivalent to an ad valorem tariff of 24 per cent at 1992 unit values); for imports above this threshold, the duty increased to Ecu 850 per tonne (206 per cent ad valorem equivalent).

The object of the two-tier tariff was to allow the Latin American countries to continue to supply their traditional share of the market while imposing a serious barrier to attempts to increase their market share at the expense of preferred suppliers. Caribbean and African suppliers no longer have an absolute advantage in the UK and French markets, but they have a substantial tariff advantage provided that the Latin American tariff quota has been set at a level that will leave space for them.

An additional feature of the new regime, which fuelled much of the subsequent controversy, was the introduction of three types of licence for importers of the two million tonne quota for dollar fruit. The reason for this innovation was that the new regime was expected to lead to a fall in prices in the protected markets and an increase in price in the free markets. The companies engaged in supplying the former argued, successfully, that their profit margins would be eroded. The licenses were designed to allow them to make profits in the free market in order to achieve a rate of return overall that would enable them to continue to ship Caribbean and African fruit. One consequence, of course, was that the traditional suppliers of dollar fruit found themselves with unwelcome new competitors in their traditional back yard.

The GATT complaint

The dollar fruit exporters were concerned both by the imposition for the first time of a tariff on exports to Germany and, more particularly, by the size of the quota to which the low tariff applied and the punitive nature of the high tariff. They claimed that the tariff quota of two million tonnes was insufficient. Five of the aggrieved Latin American exporters lodged two complaints in the GATT (one in relation to each of the EU's regulations). They were supported in their action by the USA which was concerned, at a critical time in the final negotiations of the Uruguay Round of trade liberalisation, not to permit the EU to move in the opposite direction by increasing tariffs and introducing new quotas at a time of 'tariffication'.

The GATT panel ruled in the Latin American States' favour on both complaints. Since the EU had justified its actions in relation to the Banana Protocol of the Lomé Convention, the panel in these rulings moved beyond the specific case of bananas to comment on the

GATT-compatibility of the entire Lomé Convention. This brought the spotlight of international trade law into the rather murky area of EU policy making. The GATT panel argument was that the Banana Protocol could not be supported under Article XXIV (which covers the creation of FTAs and customs unions) because there was no provision in the Lomé Convention for the eventual creation of an FTA or customs union between the contracting parties. Indeed, one of the hallmarks of the Lomé Convention is non-reciprocity. Nor could the Lomé Convention, argued the panel, be justified under the 1979 Enabling Clause (which deals with special and differential treatment of developing countries), since it is not available to all developing countries, only to a select group of them, and effectively discriminates between one set of developing countries and another set.

This view was not immediately put to the test because a compromise was agreed between the EU and the main Latin American banana exporters. Under a 'Framework Agreement on Bananas' reached in mid-1994 with four of the GATT complainants (Costa Rica, Colombia, Nicaragua, and Venezuela), the EU agreed to raise the tariff quota and to grant the four Latin American countries specific quotas based on their past share of the market. In return, the four dropped their GATT complaint.

Another feature of the deal was that the four Latin American States were authorised to issue export licences, i.e. to determine which suppliers could take advantage of the EU's import licences. This was seen by them as enhancing their negotiating position vis-à-vis the US companies that have dominated the trade in dollar fruit to Europe.

The WTO complaint

This agreement stirred up, in turn, its own controversy. It was rejected by other Latin American suppliers (including Guatemala, which had been party to the GATT complaint, plus Ecuador, Honduras, Panama, Mexico, and the Dominican Republic). Guatemala indicated that it would

continue its action.

The agreement was also opposed by two US banana companies that felt discriminated against by the overall tariff quota, by the country quotas for the four Latin American signatories and by increased competition with other companies. The decision to allocate part of the 'free market' in Europe to Geest and Fyffes (the traditional suppliers of Caribbean fruit), together with the Latin American agreement that linked the allocation of licences to the possession of an export certificate issued by the Latin American State concerned, restricted the traditional activities of United Fruit and Standard Fruit. The companies sought action from the US government, which responded by launching an investigation under Section 301 of the US trade act and then lodging a complaint in the WTO.

The WTO panel issued a report in May 1997 which upheld the complaint. Importantly, the report did not take issue with the duty-free preferences for the ACP, but found fault with aspects of the licensing system. The EU appealed, but the appellate body upheld the panel's decision. A subsequent dispute in the autumn of 1998 between the USA and the EU over whether the latter's policy changes agreed after the appeal ruling dealt adequately with the complaint only added to the reverberations. Although targeted at one product, the dispute has much wider implications.

The impact on the Lomé Convention

Whilst it did not result in a fundamental challenge to the Lomé Convention's multilateral legitimacy, the banana dispute had two major effects on EU thinking:

❖ it established that the EU's trade agreements could no longer be passed 'on the nod', and would need to be justified in the multilateral fora;

❖ it demonstrated that the WTO's new, more muscular dispute settlement procedures could throw unwanted light into murky corners of EU policy and bring into question arrangements and understandings not directly related to the point at issue.

This second point (not yet fully digested) may turn out with hindsight to be the most important. An argument made by the EU in its defence in the WTO complaint was that the quotas were justified in its Uruguay Round tariff schedules. By ruling that provisions in the schedules could not be sustained if they contravened fundamental WTO principles, the judgement could open the way to further challenges in other areas (such as the Sugar Protocol).

Over the decades since Lomé I the ACP have become less important for the EU, but the power of inertia allowed the Convention to continue largely unchanged. The banana disputes showed with frightening clarity that, rather than being just an irrelevance, the Convention could prove to be a serious embarrassment. This provided a stimulus to find a new formulation that would remove the danger.

The initial response to the challenge presented to the Lomé Convention was for the EU to seek and obtain in 1994 a waiver from the MFN rule under GATT Article XXV. This removed the immediate questions about the validity of the Lomé Convention. But while the waiver, since renewed by the WTO, has provided some respite, the problem has not gone away.

The options

The task is to transform Lomé (and the EU's other accords) so that they are permissible under one of the provisions which enable members to seek justification for discriminatory treatment of one group of trading countries vis-B-vis others (which is what preferences are). These are:

❖   if the countries concerned are creating an FTA or customs union (covered by Article XXIV);

❖   if the trade partners are developing countries subject to 'special and differential treatment' (covered by the 1979 Enabling Clause);

❖   if a waiver has been obtained under WTO Article IX (formerly GATT Article XXV).

Article XXIV

The formal procedure for obtaining WTO approval for an FTA is fairly straightforward. Two salient requirements of Article XXIV are that the FTA must be completed 'within a reasonable length of time' (newly defined in the WTO as a period that 'should exceed ten years only in exceptional cases') and that 'duties and other restrictive regulations of commerce . . . are eliminated on substantially all the trade between the constituent territories' (GATT 1947: Part 3, Article XXIV, paras 5(c) and 8(b); WTO 1995: 32). The parties to the agreement should notify the WTO following signature.

Under the GATT, notification was generally followed by the establishment of a working group (membership of which was open to any country that felt it to be in their interests to belong) which produced a report that should then be adopted by consensus by the Council. This practice is set to continue under the WTO. The majority of the cases notified to the GATT were interim agreements, some of the provisions of which came into effect before the relevant working group had completed its deliberations.

It would appear, therefore, that to be accepted by the WTO an FTA requires universal approval (because of the practice of achieving consensus). However, during the time of the GATT this was rarely achieved. As of January 1995, a total of 98 agreements had been notified under Article XXIV, but only six (of which only two are still operative) had been explicitly acknowledged as being in conformity with Article XXIV. In other words, the formal requirements for legitimisation of an FTA are high, but in the past a failure to achieve these has not proved to be a barrier to those countries wishing to create one.

The current procedure following the successful completion of an FTA is for it to be referred to the WTO Committee on Regional

Agreements for consideration. This committee has a large backlog of agreements: it is still assessing accords notified before the completion of the Uruguay Round (and hence subject to GATT rules), and so has not yet begun to establish any guidance for the interpretation of the regulations under the WTO. On past form, it is unlikely to give a straightforward approval or disapproval of any agreement.

In the absence of clear guidance from the committee, it would still be open to any aggrieved WTO member to file a complaint under the dispute settlement mechanism. For example, if the USA considered that an EU–South Africa FTA disadvantaged its exporters, it might post a complaint. But this would be risky. There is very little guidance available on how the weasel words of Article XXIV are to be interpreted. As the banana dispute has shown, the WTO has given birth to a strong dispute settlement mechanism. Any country launching a complaint would have to weigh up the possible consequences of multilateral trade policy being established in a quasi judicial framework rather than through inter-governmental negotiation. This 'case law' could have far-reaching implications and some of these might rebound on the complainant in unexpected ways.

On the other hand, the USA is not the only country that could lodge a complaint – any WTO member might do so. And not all countries facing trade diversion in either the South African or the EU market will necessarily attach much weight to the danger of a precedent being established. So any accord could be vulnerable to challenge.

In short, it is far from clear what the response in the WTO would be to any post-Lomé REPA, but the reception of the EU–South Africa FTA may show the way. This agreement which, if the negotiations do not collapse, will be completed well in advance of the REPAs, is likely to be of such commercial importance for third parties that they will have to consider carefully their reaction to it. It is partly for this reason that it is considered in Part 2 of this report. Once a precedent has been set, it is likely that it will be applied to less commercially important agreements such as the REPAs.

Special and differential treatment

The main problem with any EU attempt to justify any of its preferential accords other than the Standard GSP in relation to the 1979 Enabling Clause is that they do not cover all developing countries. In this respect, therefore, Lomé is no different from the bilateral accords that have not yet been transformed into FTAs and, arguably, the Super GSP, given that it is not limited to a recognised group of especially poor countries.

It would seem impossible to overcome this limitation, unless either the liberality of the Lomé preferences were extended to all countries or they were reduced to the level currently available under the GSP, or something in between. The first seems very unlikely, since the EU has given no indication of a political willingness to extend deep preferences to the more competitive, larger developing countries. Any generalisation would tend, therefore, to be downward. This would not only erode the ACP's margin of preference, but would also effectively increase the EU's absolute level of protection.

A waiver

The third option is the one adopted by the EU in 1994: to seek a waiver from the MFN rule under Article XXV of GATT/Article IX of WTO. A majority of the 28 waivers granted since the inception of GATT have involved preferences granted by developed to developing countries on a non-reciprocal basis. The Marrakech Agreement has made more onerous the rules for approving a waiver than was the case under GATT (when the Lomé waiver was agreed). The level of support required for approval of a waiver has been increased from a two-thirds majority under the GATT to a 75 per cent majority under the WTO. Nonetheless, the provision is well used. Both the USA and Canada, for example, justify their preference agreements with the Caribbean in this way.

The evolution of WTO rules

Hence all three options present problems. There is no automatic right to discriminate under an FTA. Each FTA must be accepted by consensus of the WTO's members. Since they will discriminate against the ACP's other trade partners (by giving the EU preferential access), they could be opposed by powerful WTO members like the USA. The 1979 Enabling Clause is ruled out as an option unless the EU is willing to extend Lomé preferences to all developing countries. Article IX requires a two-thirds majority. This is a major hurdle but, it is important to note, is less onerous than the consensus requirement for FTAs under Article XXIV. In practice the political, as opposed to the arithmetical, requirements of both are probably identical: neither could be pushed through over the opposition of major States. It is an open question which of the two would be more likely to provoke such opposition.

Since WTO compatibility represents a problem for any successor to Lomé (as well as for several of the EU's other accords), any successful outcome will have to be negotiated. Any claim by the EU that one route (e.g. REPAs) is problem-free is unfounded. It remains open to the ACP to propose alternatives. These could widen the discussion to include possible amendments to WTO rules.

It is important to keep a clear hold of the chronology of the Lomé renegotiation and other relevant policy discussions. The period to the year 2000 is intended to establish a Framework Agreement for EU–ACP relations; the details of any post-Lomé accord will not be thrashed out until the period 2000–2005. The WTO agenda is not yet certain, but there are some moves to launch a Millennium Round of negotiations covering a wide range of subjects. It is also possible that some contracting parties may become alarmed by the genie of dispute settlement uncorked fro1d reformulated rules in the WTO. To be successful any moves to change WTO rules would have to be acceptable to a broad range of the membership. They would probably need, therefore, to be of value to several existing North–South preferential accords, and could not be narrowly tailored to preserve just ACP advantages over other developing countries. But it ought to be possible to identify a formulation that would, at least, make the EU–ACP relationship more secure whilst also fitting into a broader pattern of North–South trade diplomacy.

One outcome of the Uruguay Round was to begin a process, which many expect to continue, of changing special and differential treatment in relation to non-least-developed developing countries. The Ruggiero proposal to 'bind' GSP rates for LDDCs has taken this evolution of special and differential a step further. It might be most appropriate to consider any reformulation of existing rules to accommodate better North–South preferences in the context of this process of redefinition of special and differential treatment. The onus is on the ACP to negotiate not only with the EU but, probably more importantly, other developing countries and other industrialised States with preferential trade deals outside the GSP (such as USA and Canada) to develop a consensus in favour of such change.

The Stimulus from Liberalisation

Lomé's place in EU trade policy

Lomé is now only one element of the EU's wider trade policy system. This provides different degrees of preference to various groups of countries, developed and developing. It is not only in Lomé that preferences are unrelated to the beneficiary's level of development.

There are at least five bands in this hierarchy, or more if the Europe Agreements are considered as a separate category (Figure 1). These include, in addition to Lomé, the bilateral agreements that the EU has with over 30 States, the superior layer of the GSP (the 'Super' GSP), the standard GSP and, the bottom tier, MFN, terms.

Since the first three of these bands have much in common and are distinguishable as a broader grouping from the bottom two bands it is helpful to think of the EU's trade policy as defining three groups of States. Each of these is of roughly equal importance in trade terms since each accounted for approximately one-third of European imports in 1995. They are:

❖ the 121 developed, developing and transition States that fall into the three top bands of the hierarchy and receive most favourable access;

❖ the newly industrialised, middle-income and poor countries that benefit only from the standard GSP, numbering some 54;

❖ the industrialised States that receive the misnamed *most*-favoured-nation treatment by virtue of their WTO membership, together with States that are not in the WTO but to which the EU offers autonomously MFN access, which in fact receive least favourable access.

All ACP States are in the first group and hence are treated broadly the same as Europe's Southern and Eastern neighbours and the Andean States. If all or some of the ACP were transferred to the GSP they would face discrimination vis-à-vis the other 'top group' States, many of which are richer than most of the Lomé States. But even if there is no transfer out of Lomé, the value to the ACP of their preferences will be reduced if there are any improvements to the other tiers.

Key features of the GSP

The present GSP for industrial products was introduced in 1995 and will expire in 2004. Following the Uruguay Round's emphasis on tariff-only protection, the tariff quotas and ceilings of the previous GSP were replaced by 'tariff modulation' on most industrial products (Chapters 25 to 99), with the exclusions of some primary products, leather products, steel, aluminium, lead and some other metals (Annex IX).

Tariff modulation takes the form of four lists of products detailed in Annex I of the scheme.

❖ The first list of products is described as 'very sensitive' and provides for only a 15 per cent reduction in tariffs. All textiles and clothing products covering Chapters 60 to 63 are included in this section, together with Chapter 52 covering cotton and some other products such as ferro-alloys.

❖ The second list, of sensitive products, provides for a 30 per cent reduction in

Figure 1 The EU's trade policy hierachy

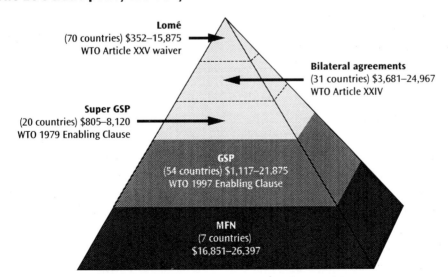

Figures illustrate lower and upper *per capita* GDP range of countries in group, based on UNDP *Human Development Report 1997* (PP$ 1994)

tariffs and covers an extensive list of products such as chemicals, rubber tyres, hides and skins, leather clothing, plywood and veneers, footwear, ceramics, metal goods, electrical and electronic goods, bicycles and toys.

❖ The third list, of semi-sensitive products, provides for a 65 per cent reduction in tariffs and covers such goods as chemical products, white goods, machinery, electrical and electronic goods and optical goods.

❖ The fourth list, of non-sensitive products, provides duty-free access for a fairly short list including some toys, games and sports equipment and miscellaneous manufactures.

The Andean group of countries – Colombia, Venezuela, Ecuador, Peru and Bolivia – obtains duty-free access on all products covered by the scheme.

Following the Singapore Ministerial Conference of the WTO in December 1996, the EU agreed in March 1998 to extend the coverage of the GSP for the least-developed countries (which already received duty-free access for all products covered by the scheme) to include all products currently excluded from it but exempt from customs duties under Lomé.

Preferences for **agricultural products** cover a more limited range of products than for industrial products. There are four lists of products – very sensitive, sensitive, semi-sensitive and non-sensitive –with the same levels of tariff reductions as apply to industrial products. Some of the products of relevance to existing ACP exports include:

❖ in the very sensitive list certain types of fish, cut flowers 1 June to 31 October, some fruit and vegetables, grapes, citrus fruit, fruit juices, tobacco;

❖ in the sensitive list certain types of fish, plants, dried vegetables, palm kernel oil, cocoa butter, cocoa paste, tobacco not stemmed or stripped;

❖ in the semi-sensitive list certain types of fish, shrimps and prawns, lobster, crabs, molluscs, octopus, plants, roasted coffee, vanilla, palm oil.

❖ in the non-sensitive list coffee, not roasted or decaffeinated, green tea in packs of less than 3 kg, pepper, extracts of tea.

A fifth list of products provides duty-free access for the Andean and Central American countries. This covers products under: Chapter 3 – such as fish, crustaceans, molluscs and other aquatic invertebrates (with the exception of a 3.6 per cent duty for shrimps and prawns); Chapter 6 – covering plants, cut flowers, etc.; sub-head 0708 – leguminous vegetables, tomatoes, plantains, pineapples, mangoes, citrus fruit 15 May to 15 September, pawpaws; coffee roasted or unroasted; ground nut oil; palm kernel oil; Chapter 18 – cocoa and cocoa preparations; Chapter 19 – preparations of cereals etc.; Chapter 20 – preparations of vegetables, fruit etc.; Chapter 24 – tobacco and substitutes.

There is implicitly a sixth list, of products excluded from the scheme, but unlike the offer on industrial products this is not included in the offer on agricultural products (presumably because it would be too long!).

The least-developed countries obtain tariff reductions on agricultural products in line with ACP preferences that were previously excluded from the GSP. This concession, however, only applies to agricultural products subject under the Lomé Convention to a tariff reduction but not to products subject to a tariff quota.

Special incentives are included in the scheme under the Social Clause and the Environmental Clause. The social clause covers ILO Conventions 87 and 98, the right to organise, and 28 covering the minimum age of employment. The environmental clause covers agreements on sustainable forest management. The incentive consists of a 20 per cent enhancement of benefits for the implementation of one clause and a 30 per cent enhancement for the fulfilment of both clauses, which may be granted if proof of fulfilment of the clauses is provided.

Partial **graduation** from the scheme on a product/country basis is provided for under a complex formula comprising three elements. First, a 'relative specialisation measure' – the share of the beneficiary in total EU imports of the product (defined at the tariff line). Second, adjustment of the specialisation index by an index of the level of development of the beneficiary – measured by *per capita* GNP relative to that of the EU and the level of manufactured exports relative to the EU. Third, rules for combining the two indices.

In addition, beneficiaries are excluded from the scheme on a product-by-product basis, regardless of their level of development, if EU imports of the product are greater than 25 per cent of total EU imports of the product from all beneficiaries. This rule is targeted principally at large and competitive developing countries such as China and Brazil, but could conceivably affect any country.

Finally, more developed countries with a *per capita* GNP greater than $6,000 in 1991 were graduated out of the scheme on a sector/country basis (Annex II), affecting the six Gulf States, Singapore, South Korea, Libya, Brunei and Nauru.

In addition, preferences may be suspended if the EU considers that a beneficiary has engaged in unfair trading practices, used forced labour or prison labour, or has inadequate controls over drugs and money laundering.

The abolition of tariff quotas and ceilings that featured in earlier versions of the GSP led to a more restrictive approach to the **safeguard clause** in the new GSP. In the previous Scheme the clause could be implemented only if it there was 'economic difficulty' for the EU or one of its regions. Under the current GSP this has been extended to include 'economic difficulty' to a competing EU producer. The safeguard clause is similar in its wording to GATT Article XXIV but does not invoke this GATT Article and therefore need not follow the constraints contained in the Uruguay Round Agreement on Safeguards. In addition, an emergency procedure can be introduced in 'excep-

tional circumstances'. As in the previous GSP, evidence does not have to be established of any causality between GSP imports and the 'economic difficulty' (though the European Court might regard this as implicit in the agreement).

In addition, the least-developed countries are no longer exempt from the re-imposition of tariffs under this clause.

One small improvement was the attempt to make the use of the safeguard clause a more open system by listing ten criteria that had to be met before the safeguard provisions could be implemented. These ten criteria are very widely stated, covering for example reductions in the market share of Community producers, or reductions in their production, or the closure of productive capacity, low profitability, or low rate of capacity utilisation. If these wide criteria are still insufficient, then appeals can be made to general employment, trade, or price effects.

The potentially restrictive effect of the safeguard clause in the GSP should be contrasted with the safeguard clause, Article 177, in the Lomé Convention. This can be implemented if imports 'result in serious disturbances in a sector of the economy of the Community or one or more of the Member States, or jeopardise their external stability'. These measures must be notified immediately to the Council of Ministers and the EU undertakes not to use means which hamper structural development. When applied, safeguard measures have 'to take account of the existing level of the ACP exports concerned to the Community and the potential for development'. The EU also undertakes to ensure that the safeguard measures are restricted to those which would least disturb trade with the ACP countries.

Extensions to the GSP

In its response to the Ruggiero Proposal, the EU has agreed to extend to the least-developed countries duty-free access on all industrial products and on agricultural goods that are given unrestricted duty-free access under the Lomé Convention. Since the situation with respect to these products cannot be improved upon, there is no scope for further enhancement in tariff policy for the LDDCs. There remains scope, however, to extend the tariff cuts to those agricultural products that are currently excluded, and also to improve non-tariff aspects of the LDDCs' market access (such as with respect to the rules of origin). The extension of Lomé-style preferences to LDDCs will erode ACP preference margins. If the offer to LDDCs were extended to the items currently excluded, the ACP could be put in a relatively unfavourable position.

It is possible, however, that these changes could be turned to the advantage of the ACP. It is proposed in Part 3 that a part of the ACP strategy should be the improvement of the GSP as it applies to least-developed and other vulnerable economies in order to provide an improved 'safety net' in the event that REPAs prove unpalatable (or unacceptable in the WTO). For this reason, the matter is dealt with in more detail in Part 3.

Other preference agreements

The Lomé Convention and the GSP are not the only parts of the EU pyramid of privilege that are undergoing change. In addition to proposed FTAs with Mercosur, Chile, perhaps Mexico, and even North America, the EU is renegotiating many of its Mediterranean accords. In Part 2 of the report the examples are given of the Morocco and South Africa FTAs, since these provide an illustration of what the EU may be proposing for REPAs. Probably the greatest geographical area of change is in relation to the Mediterranean.

Objectives of the Euro–Med agreements

The objectives of the Euro–Med Agreements are set out in the Barcelona Declaration of November 1995. The EU has noted that the population of the non-EU Mediterranean countries will reach 400 million by 2000 and that the relatively high rates of growth of population in these countries have produced a young age distribution of the population, and so a substantial proportion will be seeking employment. The EU is already concerned about the political stability of a region

close to its own frontiers as well as the internal political problem of migrant workers seeking employment in the EU countries. The EU therefore regards the problems of political stability and the generation of growth of output and employment in the region as an urgent problem. To quote the Barcelona Declaration, 'time is of the essence'.

In order to consolidate peace and stability in the region, three main areas have been targeted for action:

❖   support for political reform;

❖   defence of human rights;

❖   promotion of economic and social reform to:
   • increase growth and create employment;
   • increase standards of living;
   • ease migration pressure.

Decreasing the wealth gap between the EU and the Mediterranean countries is seen as essential to improving the stability of the region and three priorities for action have been identified:

❖   assistance with economic transition;

❖   assistance with achieving a better socio–economic balance;

❖   backing for regional integration.

Of these three priorities, assistance with economic transition forms the main thrust of EU action. There are four main avenues for this support:

❖   a Euro–Med FTA;

❖   promotion of the domestic private sector;

❖   promotion of European private investment;

❖   the updating of the economic and social infrastructure.

The first of these is of particular relevance to the ACP. It is clear from the content of the mandate for negotiation with the ACP countries (EU Council 1998) that the form of the proposed REPAs is to be modelled on the Euro–Med agreements, although the ACP countries will have substantial discretion in determining the content and transition to free trade.

The basic principles of the Euro–Med agreements as set out by the EU are:

❖ respect for WTO obligations;

❖ openness to any country in the region accepting the market economy.

The objective is to establish a Euro–Med FTA by 2010. Bilateral FTAs have so far been signed with Israel, Jordan, Tunisia, Morocco and the PLO, and customs union agreements have been concluded with Cyprus and Turkey. The current objectives are to conclude agreements with Egypt and Lebanon as soon as possible.

A detailed analysis of the EU–Morocco Agreement is provided in Part 3. As an exemplar of the EU's recent attitude towards FTAs it may help to flesh out the very vague references to REPAs in the Green Paper and the Negotiating Mandate. As such, it provides the ACP with guidance on what they may expect the EU to propose in any post-Lomé REPA negotiations.

Multilateral liberalisation

The Uruguay Round set in train various liberalisation exercises that will affect the value to the ACP of the Lomé provisions, and also set out a timetable for new talks on some aspects of trade policy. The two most important of these changes for the ACP relate to textiles/clothing and to temperate agriculture.

The Agreement on Textiles and Clothing

The Agreement on Textiles and Clothing, an integral part of the Uruguay Round, provides a timetable for the phased dismantling of the MFA and the full integration of the international trade in textiles and clothing into the GATT.

This is a major change, since the MFA has operated as the primary instrument of developed country protection against developing country textile and clothing exports since 1974. It has provided a free-standing multilateral framework for the proliferation of discriminatory quantitative restrictions against 35 developing countries and economies in transition[3] in clear violation of the spirit of the GATT, from which it was an agreed derogation. Many developing countries rely heavily on textiles and clothing, which are relatively labour intensive and account for a much higher share of their exports than its six per cent share of world merchandise trade.

Under the Agreement on Textiles and Clothing, all bilaterally agreed and MFA-based quantitative restrictions are to be notified to the Textiles Monitoring Board for removal according to a graduated schedule, with expanded quotas in the interim. Any restrictions inconsistent with the GATT are to be notified and brought into conformity with the GATT.

The MFA restrictions are to be phased out over ten years in a process that began in 1995. The phase-out contains two key components plus a relaxation of restrictions on transfers between over- and under-utilised quotas:

❖ **Re-integration:** quotas are to be abolished in four stages, of which two have been completed and the remainder end in 2002 and 2005. During each a minimum number of textile and clothing items will be re-integrated into GATT rules, based on 1990 import volumes. The shares for the two remaining phases are: 18 per cent and a full 49 per cent which is to be re-integrated only at the end. Products from each category (tops, yarns, fabrics, made-up textiles and

---

3   China, Hong Kong, Macao and the Republic of Korea appear the most targeted partners. Restrictions have also been applied to non-MFA members such as Taiwan, some Eastern European countries and China (until 1992). The principal developed countries involved in textile and clothing restrictions are the USA, the EU and Canada, which accounted for over 70 per centpercent of MFA bilateral agreements.

Australia and Norway (occasional MFA participants) and New Zealand (never an MFA member) have also applied restrictions, but not in the form of the bilateral or unilateral agreements set out in the MFA. Australia used tariff quotas and government quota auctioning. Norway applied a global quota. Switzerland, although an MFA member, never applied restraints but instead used a price surveillance system on imports.

clothing) have to be re-integrated in every stage, but no minimum has been set for each group.

❖ **Quota acceleration:** In the two remaining stages annual quota growth rates are to increase by 25 per cent and 27 per cent respectively. Small suppliers whose exports accounted in 1991 for 1.2 per cent or less of 'the total volume of restrictions applied by an importing country' (e.g. Peru and Sri Lanka in the case of the EU) were granted higher quota growth rates. Between 1994 and 2004, volumes of EU imports subject to quotas would increase by 64 per cent through the application of quota growth factors.

Since the quota growth rates are based on the existing country quotas, which were not based on either developmental or efficiency criteria, existing disparities between developing countries will remain and widen during the re-integration period.

The Agreement on Textiles and Clothing has not yet had a big impact, and may not result in a significant liberalisation for developing exporters until 2005. Integration is heavily endloaded: restrictions on items accounting for almost half of the 1990 volume of trade do not need to be removed until the final 2005 deadline. Since importing countries have discretion over the product mix of each tranche, items of most commercial significance and subject to the heaviest protection, such as clothing, are likely to be delayed for as long as possible.

None of the ten products selected by the EU in the first stage of integration had previously been subject to EU quantitative restrictions, and a number of the product groups listed by the EU as fully integrated were in fact only partially de-restricted. As a result, although the tranche fulfilled the Agreement on Textiles and Clothing

target (set at 16 per cent of the *volume* of imports) its share by *value* of EU imports was only half this level (8.7 per cent of total and 7.8 per cent of developing country originating imports).[4] The EU made greater progress in the second stage, in which clothing items such as workwear, ski suits and woven gloves were re-integrated.

On one estimate, 67 per cent of the EU's Agreement on Textiles and Clothing imports from the non-industrialised countries remain to be re-integrated (Baughman *et al.*, 1997). For some exporters the proportion is much higher: between 81 per cent and 91 per cent of all the EU's textile and clothing imports from Hong Kong, Morocco, Tunisia and Macau are still to be liberalised.

The manner in which integration targets have been met also runs contrary to the spirit if not the letter of the Agreement on Textiles and Clothing. The EU included in its integration schedule a large number of non-textile and non-clothing products that happened to contain textile components, such as umbrellas, car seat belts and parachutes. Such items accounted for a full 58 per cent of the EU's first-stage integration schedule, but were less in evidence in the second stage.

Assessing the possible impact

The MFA protected developed country industry (and penalised their consumers) by artificially restricting supply, thereby raising prices, through quotas. The Agreement on Textiles and Clothing will reverse these effects. Because consumers will gain from falling prices, trade liberalisation has been wholeheartedly supported by European consumer associations.

Although developed country producers will face increased competition, the textile industry is already having to adjust to a decline in the share of consumer expenditure on clothing. Strategies favoured by the industry include greater specialisation, outward processing, and

---

4   The ATC volume figure (and hence also the value figures cited) are in relation to 1990 imports.

the production of high-quality technical textiles adapted to consumer demands and changes in fashion.

The pattern of exports will also change, creating winners and losers. The MFA has restricted exporting countries to different degrees creating a trade pattern that is unlikely to mirror their relative efficiency, or that of firms within them. Furthermore, the combination of strong protection with liberal preferences for some suppliers has led to a diversion of imports to less protected, but possibly less efficient, foreign suppliers. In the EU's case these are the ACP, and also the Mediterranean and Central and Eastern European (CEEC) trade partners.

Quantifying the impact on winners and losers is complex and controversial because it requires information on the characteristics of supply and demand as well as the calculation of tariff equivalents for each product quota. General equilibrium models have been used to simulate the economy-wide changes that will result from the Agreement on Textiles and Clothing. They differ in their characteristics and assumptions, and hence in their results.

One illustrative simulation up to 2005 finds that many Asian suppliers will gain from the Agreement on Textiles and Clothing (Hertel *et al.*, 1996: Table 7.9). Southeast and South Asia gain markedly as, potentially, does China. Malaysia loses from a re-deployment to other industrial sectors (in particular towards the food industry).

Losers include the Asian Newly Industrialised Economies (NIEs). This is because although exporters faced tight MFA restrictions their quotas also guaranteed some minimum market access and protection from newer and more efficient suppliers. Increased competition and their own diversification away from textile and clothing production is expected to produce a substantial welfare loss from the MFA abolition.

Sub-Saharan African (and, by implication, other ACP) exporters are also expected to suffer from the MFA abolition because of preference erosion. Exports to the EU may be displaced by Asian suppliers, and any that remain will suffer deteriorating terms of trade as prices in the liberalised markets fall. Although current exports are modest, these expectations cast a shadow over hopes to develop the sector.

The Agreement on Agriculture

Agriculture, one of the most contentious issues, was included in the Uruguay Round because there was 'an urgent need to bring more discipline and predictability to world agricultural trade by correcting and preventing restrictions and distortions' (Croome, 1995). The chief sponsor of reform was the USA; 'most of the Western European countries, Japan, Korea and a large number of the smaller developing countries were broadly on the defensive throughout' [*ibid.*].

One result was that, while the Agreement began the process of establishing a framework of trade rules for agriculture similar to what exists for manufactures, it did not complete the task. In recognition of this, it agreed that negotiations for continuing the process 'will be initiated one year before the end of the implementation period' of the Uruguay Round commitments (Article 20). This is conventionally taken to mean the turn of the century.

The Agreement on Agriculture reformed the main forms of subsidy. The complex pattern of direct and indirect subsidies has been sorted into two categories:

❖ *consumer subsidies*: indirect transfers from consumers to producers through artificially high prices, usually induced by supply restrictions (such as tariffs and quotas on imports and domestic production);

❖ *producer or taxpayer subsidies*: direct and indirect transfers from government to producers (such as EU intervention buying and export subsidies).

The Uruguay Round agreed cuts to both types of subsidy, and established differential treatment for developing countries.

Tariffs

Industrial States must reduce tariffs by 36 per cent over six years, while developing countries have to do so by 24 per cent over ten years: the least-developed do not need to cut their tariffs.

Production subsidies

Aggregate producer subsidies are to be cut by 20 per cent by industrialised countries over six years, and by 13.3 per cent by developing countries over the same period, but not by least-developed States.

Export subsidies

Developed countries must reduce by 36 per cent the *value* of their direct export subsidies and by 21 per cent the *quantity* of subsidised exports over six years. The cuts for developing countries are set at two-thirds this level over ten years. No cuts need be made by least-developed States. The reduction in import barriers is being implemented through two instruments:

- ❖ the conversion of all import restrictions into tariffs (a process known as tariffication);

- ❖ and guarantees of a certain level of market access and the reduction and binding of tariffs.

In order to establish subsidy reduction targets, the Uruguay Round negotiated a method of linking the many different varieties into a controversial Aggregate Measure of Support (AMS) which allows various exemptions. Producer subsidies were classified into groups to determine whether or not they needed to be reduced and whether action could be taken against them under the WTO's dispute settlement mechanism. They are:

- ❖ The Green Box: supports to agriculture which are deemed to be non, or minimally, trade distorting. They do not need to be reduced under the Round and, under the so-called Peace Clause (Article 13), other WTO members cannot take action against them (such as the imposition of countervailing duties).

- ❖ The Special and Differential Box: exempts from reduction investment and agricultural input subsidies generally available to developing country agriculture and low-income farmers, as well as anti-narcotic diversification incentives.

- ❖ The Blue Box: direct payments under 'production limiting' programmes need not be cut but may be actionable by other WTO members.

Impact on developing countries

Developing countries (and socio–economic groups within them) will be affected by these changes:

- ❖ indirectly via the impact of subsidy removal on the world market (leading to a rise in prices and, possibly, reduction of supply);

- ❖ directly by any constraints on their own action to develop agriculture *inter alia* to address the new opportunities and challenges.

The indirect impact will depend upon each producer's status as a net importer or exporter and capacity to alter supply and demand. If liberalisation boosts world prices it will tend to benefit net exporters and penalise net importers. Exporters that can increase supply to take advantage of the higher prices will gain most. Importers that are able to boost domestic production will be able to mitigate the costs (or even become net exporters), while those that cannot will bear the brunt of the adjustment.

A complicating factor arises from the co-existence of heavy agricultural protectionism with substantial trade preferences for favoured suppliers, such as under the EU's Lomé and Mediterranean accords. As explained in the next section, on the CAP, because preference beneficiaries receive prices related to those in the high-cost, protected markets, rather than the world price, they will see their export prices drop as a result of liberalisation. This will cause particular problems to high-cost exporters (such as Caribbean sugar producers), with limited scope to increase the volume of output (to offset falling unit values) or to cut the cost of production.

The next Round

While the direct effects of the Agreement on Agriculture are not great, the same will not necessarily be true of its successor. Also, the ACP and other developing countries will be affected indirectly by what others agree. Hence, a continuation of the *status quo* is not an option. Since the WTO operates by consensus the ACP have the opportunity to influence both the agenda and the outcome, but this is a resource-intensive process which few, if any, ACP countries can complete successfully acting alone.

It is not easy to predict the speed at which multilateral trade talks will progress, particularly in difficult areas such as agriculture, but developing countries need to start preparing soon. There are two key dates, 2000 and 2003, although these provide only a partial indicator. The Agreement on Agriculture States that new negotiations will commence one year before the end of the implementation period. This is generally taken to imply a formal start at the end of 1999 or early in 2000. The so-called 'Peace Clause' expires in 2003. This limits challenges to subsidies in the Green Box. Its expiry will make some subsidies – notably many of the EU's – vulnerable to petitions for WTO Dispute Settlement.

Other factors that are likely to influence the speed, breadth and success of the negotiations are:

❖ whether parallel multilateral talks get under way on, for example, trade in

industrial products, or on the *new* areas of intellectual property, competition and services;

❖ the speed of internally generated EU reform linked to enlargement and the budget;

❖ the economic situation in other major economic actors that protect their agriculture, such as Japan.

Although it is premature to speculate about the details of the agenda, it is likely that there will be pressure for it to include:

❖ a further reduction on tariffs (which are still high);

❖ further cuts in AMS, and the extension of reductions to subsidies currently in the Green and Blue Boxes;

❖ further erosion of special and differential treatment for developing countries.

The main protagonists are already positioning themselves. The USA's FAIR Act of 1996 has reorganised the provision of agricultural subsidies in such a way as to make them more compatible with the rubric of the Agreement on Agriculture. This may allow it to press hard for large AMS cuts, a position likely to be endorsed by the Cairns Group.[5]

The Stimulus of Common Agricultural Policy Reform

The EU's *Agenda 2000* plan serves to prepare for the next Round as well as:

❖ limiting production of certain products which the EU fears will otherwise cause it difficulty in meeting its commitments to reduce the volume of subsidised exports without expensive and politically unacceptable action such as stockpiling;

---

5   Fourteen states that account for about one-quarter of world agricultural exports, and only lightly protect and subsidise their agriculture. The members of the Cairns Group are: Argentina, Australia, Brazil, Canada, Chile, Colombia, Fiji, Indonesia, Malaysia, Philippines, New Zealand, South Africa, Thailand and Uruguay.

- restraining agricultural spending at a time of financial stringency in all member States;

- amending the CAP so that it does not prove an obstacle to the eastward enlargement of the EU.

Because of this range of factors requiring reform, change in the CAP is likely to occur outside as well as inside the WTO. This is important for the ACP because the CAP has had a profound and complex impact on them, as well as other developing countries. This has been the result of both positive and negative effects on different products, countries and time periods. As the CAP is reformed, so these effects will change. The combination of simultaneous change to the CAP and to preferences could have substantial effects on some ACP countries.

How the CAP affects developing countries

Five potential effects on developing countries of the complex CAP regimes are identified in Table 3. Measuring any of these effects accurately presents methodological problems, which are especially severe when attention is focused on particular commodities or third parties. But, except in the case of price instability, a *broad indication* of the countries most likely to be affected and the potential scale of any effect can be obtained from an analysis of trade data. Moreover, even though it is difficult to hang accurate figures on them, it is possible to identify those aspects of the CAP that produce the effects noted. By the same token, it is feasible to categorise the proposed and possible reforms to the CAP in terms of the direction of their likely impact.

The chains of effect

The literature has established that there is a need for a range of analyses (from dynamic, economy-wide studies to product-specific, static ones), depending on the circumstances of the issues being addressed. This section focuses on the specific ways in which the changes to the CAP that are anticipated in the short term will affect particular sets of developing countries and socio–economic groups within them.

For this purpose, and because the indirect effects of the CAP on third parties may be as great as the direct impact, it is helpful to think of 'chains of effect' with several inter-mediate links. These are illustrated schematically in Tables 4, 5 and 6, which deal with its impact:

- on world supply;

- on EU prices;

- and on heavily subsidised exports.

Table 3. Types of CAP effect on developing countries

Type of effect	Positive features	Negative features	Implications for development policy
Increased world supply	Lowers import costs for importers (and may increase supply of food aid)	Lowers export prices for exporters Disincentive to agricultural development of importers and exporters	May undermine agricultural development policies, but also reduces food costs
Artificially high EU prices	Artificially high prices for developing countries able to export (e.g. because of Lomé Protocols)	Exports may be viable only if high prices continue	May support export diversification, but new exports may be unsustainable
Over-subsidised prices of exports	Lowers import costs for importers	May undermine domestic agriculture and disrupt legitimate trade	May undermine agricultural development policies
Increased world price instability		Increases food insecurity and complicates agricultural development planning	Disrupts long-term agricultural development

Increased world supply

The most fundamental of the CAP effects is its impact on world supply (Table 4). There is widespread agreement that, since the CAP results in levels of EU production that are higher than would have occurred in its absence and given that the EU is a substantial producer, it follows that world production is also increased unless, of course, the additional European output is offset wholly by declines elsewhere (which is unlikely). This results in world prices being lower than they would otherwise have been.

This lowering of world prices is transmitted to developing countries (and other third parties) through a variety of mechanisms. The relative importance of each varies according to the product and, sometimes, the trade partner concerned, so that the 'real world' is much more complex than appears in Table 4. However, two important points that Table 4 is intended to convey are:

❖ that the fundamental reason for the CAP's impact on third parties is that it has increased world supply, with the transmission mechanisms being a secondary element in the picture;

❖ policy changes that alter the transmission mechanisms may nonetheless have an impact, for good or ill, on third parties even if they do not influence the fundamental CAP change.

One way in which the fall in world prices is transmitted to third parties is through the closure to them of the European market. Since the EU represents a substantial proportion of the world's consumers, the loss of this market is significant. In many cases, this will represent the most important single mechanism of transmission.

In some cases (such as cereals) the EU market is substantially closed to imports. In others (such as fruit and vegetables) it is only partly closed, and so the effects illustrated in Table 4 may be combined with the offsetting effects illustrated in Table 5. This, in turn, complicates the task of assessing overall impact in the real world.

EU exports, with and without subsidy, transmit the CAP change to third markets. Other exporting countries face greater competition in third markets than would otherwise be the case, as may domestic producers.

The implications of these changes for third-party *States* depends on whether they are exporters or importers or both. Clearly, net exporters earn less foreign exchange from trade than they otherwise would and, by the same token, net importers pay less for their food supplies.

The effects on *groups within States* will depend partly upon their status as consumers or producers of competitive products, but also on the policies of their governments. There is a range of interventions that importing governments can undertake that will offset any negative

Table 4. The chain of effect – increased world supply

Fundamental CAP change		
EU production higher	→ world production higher (unless offset)	→ world prices lower

Main effects
1. Reduced EU demand for third-party exports.
2. 'Commercial' EU exports → lower prices.
3. 'Subsidised' EU exports → ? much lower prices.

Implications	
Exporters:	lose revenue through:
	• absence from EU market;
	• lower prices in third markets;
	• subsidised competition in third markets.
Importers:	gain revenue through:
	• lower import prices.

effects of, for example, increased competition from EU exports on domestic production. These include maintaining tariffs at a level that offsets the subsidy, using countervailing duties, or providing incentives to domestic producers.

High EU prices

One of the fundamental mechanisms through which the CAP has supported European farmers is by restricting supply on to the domestic market in order to maintain prices at higher levels than otherwise would apply. This fundamental mechanism has had effects that, when combined with trade policy, are additional to those arising from the impact on world supply.

The ways in which the restriction of EU supply produces implications for third parties are illustrated in Table 5. Supply restrictions relate both to controls on domestic output (such as production quotas) and to measures designed to restrict imports (such as high tariffs and regulations that specify the minimum price for imports). In all cases, the volume of imports is lower than it would otherwise have been, but the price paid by consumers is higher (although how much of this accrues to the various elements in the supply chain – supermarkets/ importers/shippers/exporters – will vary between product, supplier and buyer).

Trade preferences can have a very important effect in relation to products controlled in this way. These take the form of:

❖ special quotas that allow some third parties to supply the high-priced EU market without paying the substantial import duties that either exclude other imports or reduce drastically their profitability (e.g. the Lomé Beef and Sugar Protocols, which provide highly preferential access for a quota set in relation to each beneficiary);

❖ preferences that relieve some third parties from a part of the price maintenance provisions and therefore increase their ability to compete with less-favoured imports (e.g. the tariff reductions on fruit and vegetables available under Lomé, the Super GSP and most bilateral agreements).

The effect of the combined import restriction and preference is to limit the volume of imports (thereby maintaining prices) but to discriminate in favour of some third-party suppliers at the expense of others. The impact of these changes on any given country depends both on its preferential status and on its ability to increase competitive supply.

The arrangements are most beneficial to those third parties that (a) receive preferences and (b) would not be able to sell larger volumes on the EU market even if it were unrestricted. Hence, for example, the high-price Caribbean sugar producers benefit greatly from the Sugar

Table 5. The chain of effect – high EU prices

Fundamental CAP change		
EU supply restricted (domestic quotas, import controls)	→ higher prices lower sales volume	→ world demand lower

Main effects
1. Volume of imports lower.
2. Price received for imports higher.
3. Preferences are very important.

Implications
Preferred exporters: earn 'surplus' profits (but exports *may* be lower than potential)
Other exporters: may also earn 'surplus' BUT lose revenue to less efficient producers whether preferred exporters or EU producers.

Protocol: they receive artificially high prices for their exports and are not adversely affected by the volume limitation since they have a limited capacity to increase their output. Were the CAP to be reformed totally, the sugar industry in most of the Caribbean States would almost certainly collapse as they could not compete on a free market.

The most adversely affected third parties are the competitive producers that do not receive preferences. In the sugar case, for example, this would include the Philippines, which not only gains no advantage from the high EU prices (because it cannot export to Europe) but also faces lower world prices as a result of the chain of effect portrayed in Table 4. In the case of fruit and vegetables, South Africa might be considered to be adversely affected, since major competitors such as Israel have preferential access to Europe.

In the middle are countries that are preferred but are also competitive producers. In such cases, it is uncertain without a detailed analysis whether they gain more on the 'swings' of high EU prices than they lose on the 'roundabouts' of volume limitation. To take the sugar example, Zimbabwe would be in this category: it has a small quota under the Lomé Sugar Protocol and is a globally efficient producer that undoubtedly could increase its exports to Europe were the import regime to be relaxed.

Over-subsidised prices

The EU has been accused of disrupting domestic agricultural production and trade in some developing country regions not just through its general effect on supply but through specific instances of extremely low-priced exports. The case of beef in West Africa hit the headlines in 1993. South Africa and Namibia have expressed recent concern about the pricing of beef exports to Southern Africa, as a result of which the EU changed their classification for refund purposes in January 1997, resulting in an 8 per cent reduction in refunds. As both cases illustrate, the EU is able to take action when market disruption has

been identified and its attention drawn to it clearly. This ability to change serves to emphasise the need for an adequate monitoring and dispute settlement system.

The fundamental problem arises, as is illustrated in Table 6, in cases where the EU's production exceeds domestic consumption. The Union is responsible for disposing of part of these surpluses, and it chooses to do this by giving exporters financial incentives to enable them to sell goods they have purchased at the high EU price on the lower-priced world market. In cases where a subsidy is required, there is always the possibility that it will be set at a level that is greater than that needed by exporters to achieve a sale on the world market.

The problem is particularly acute in the case of beef because of the fragmented nature of the world market and because of the many quality differences that are not easily measurable in a cost-effective manner by those administering the system. The former has led the EU to divide the world into nine groups of States and to offer different levels of export subsidy for each group. Countries are allocated to regions on the basis of:

❖   their interest to the EU as a market;

❖   their price levels.

Zones 8 and 9 (which equate broadly to Africa, the Middle East and the former Soviet Union, and contain a large number of the development focus States) attract the highest export refunds. In April 1997, for example, the refund for boneless cuts fresh or chilled (per 100 kg) was Ecu 94.5 for Zone 9 and Ecu 103 for Zone 8 (compared, for example, with Ecu 40 for exports to Switzerland in Zone 4).

Hence, there are particularly large refunds on exports to a high proportion of development focus States and, in addition, the effect of these subsidies on prices may be increased relatively because of the heterogeneity of beef cuts. The level of export subsidy payable on sales to a particular destination does not vary according to the quality (and hence market price) of the cut. The effect is that the proportionate reduction in price

Table 6. The chain of effect – heavily subsidised prices

Fundamental CAP change		
'Subsidised' exports	→ administered prices	→ prices unrelated to market forces

Main effects
1. Some EU exports sold at less than the cost of production in EU.
2. Some EU exports sold at less than the cost of production in a relatively efficient world producer.
3. Price levels may be erratic and have intended or unintended predatory effect.

Implications

Exporters: earn 'surplus' profits (but exports *may* be lower than potential)

Importers: • consumers pay less
  • domestic producers face 'unfair' competition

---

will be greatest for States importing the lowest-quality cuts. In extreme cases, very low-value meat may be exported. It is understood, for example, that in the case of EU beef exported to West Africa in the late 1980s and early 1990s the meat was of such low quality that the transaction was primarily of interest to traders for the export refunds; the price paid by the importing State was almost incidental.

The effects of administered export subsidies are not only that some EU exports are sold below the cost of production in the EU (which is presumably a normal state of affairs), but also that some may be sold at below the cost of production anywhere in the world. These exports are dumped in the fullest sense of the word.

The implication is that exporters cannot compete in third markets unless they are able to match the EU subsidies. WTO rules permit action to be taken against dumping. One reason for this is that it can disrupt markets both through erratic price levels and by driving legitimate, efficient producers out of business.

For importing countries, the impact depends upon whether it is consumers or domestic producers that are being considered. Evidently, consumers benefit from the subsidies paid by European taxpayers. But, unless the importing government adopts appropriate policies (such as the application of a countervailing duty), domestic producers are likely to be unable to compete with the artificially cheap imports.

The effect of reform
Scope of Agenda 2000

Agenda 2000 is primarily oriented towards the cereals, beef and oilseed sectors, with only minor reforms proposed for dairy products. The fruit and vegetables sector has been dealt with already in the reforms of 1992, and other sectors (notably sugar) are not currently causing the same level of concern in terms of meeting the EU's Uruguay Round objectives.

The broad aim in these reforms is to reduce the level of intervention prices but to offset this partially through an increase in direct income support to farmers. The ultimate objective is to enable producers to export at world market prices (with the support of adjustment aid). The Uruguay Round makes no requirements on the level of exports that are not subsidised directly.

Only in respect of cereals are the proposed intervention price cuts substantial (see Table 7). A reduction of 20 per cent by 2000 is sufficiently large and the deadline sufficiently close that, if the proposal is adopted, it could have a measurable effect. The proposed cut in beef prices is greater (at 30 per cent), but the deferral of implementation until the year 2000 onwards means that it is likely to overlap with the next round of WTO negotiations. The one may influence the other. The proposal for dairy products is, effectively, a continuation of the *status quo* until after the WTO negotiations may have been concluded.

Potential implications of change
Broad effects

There are two major problems with assessing the implications for the ACP and other developing countries of CAP reform. One is that, in the nature of things, any one set of changes will represent only a step along the road towards agriculture being treated like other areas of production.

Significantly, none of the *Agenda 2000* proposals explicitly assumes liberalisation of external trade as a concomitant of the reduction of domestic prices. This absence of explicit targets for import liberalisation from the strategic proposals being considered is important when assessing the anticipated effects as forecast by the various economic analyses. At present the ACP gain from the 'swings' of artificially high prices, even though they lose on the 'roundabouts' of restricted export volumes. If the prices are reduced without any scope to increase export volumes the effect will be wholly negative.

The second source of difficulty arises from the fact that the world has learned to live with the CAP and, hence, has adopted production and consumption patterns that are compatible with it. This applies equally to European farmers, the pattern of whose production is not necessarily the same as would apply in a market where world prices reigned. A consequence is that the task of forecasting the production and consumption response to a given set of changes is inherently speculative.

Despite these problems, it is possible to identify four different potential elements of reform. The actual impact of reform will be determined by the extent to which the actual changes fall into these categories. They are: liberalisation of market access; cuts in the volume of subsidised EU exports; the restriction of EU production; and cuts in administered European prices. These are not alternatives: any particular reform measures may involve a combination of them. But since there are clearly differing implications for third parties, and since not every step in the medium-term reform process will contain all the elements in the same proportions, it helps to clarify the direction of effect of any given set of reform proposals if the implications of each of the four elements are identified at the outset (Table 8).

As is clear from the many economic studies made of European agricultural liberalisation, there would be significant implications for third parties of any substantial removal of European import barriers. It is assumed that world prices

Table 7. The Agenda 2000 proposals[a]

Product	Proposal	Developing country effect:	
		direction	*scale*
Cereals	Intervention price cut of 20% in 2000 Set compulsory set-aside at zero	Exporters: improved exports Importers: higher import prices	Small
Beef	Intervention price cut in steps by 30% over 2000/2002	Preferred exporters: lower prices Importers: higher prices	Medium Very small
Dairy	Extend quota regime to 2006 Gradually decrease support prices by 10%	Importers: higher prices	Very small
Fruit & vegetables	No new reforms – continued implementation to shift support from prices to producer organisations	No effect	
Sugar	No proposals	-	

Note: (a) Most relevant proposals for developing countries.

would rise as a result both of increasing demand for world exports (through an opening up of the European market) and of a reduction in world supply (through the cut in European output that could be expected to result from this increased competition). This would produce a deterioration in the terms of trade of importing States. It would also produce gains for the more efficient net exporters, but its effects on less efficient world exporters are less certain. These would depend critically on the extent to which such exporters could compete at the new, lower European prices and offset the reduction in the unit value of exports with an increase in the volume. The Caribbean sugar exporters, for example, might well lose market share while the Philippines and Zimbabwe would increase theirs. Similarly, Argentina could expect to increase its exports of wheat and beef.

Liberalisation of market access is the most fundamental CAP change in the sense that its effects would be sufficiently strong to remove the need for reforms such as those considered in Table 8. These, more limited, changes are required in the absence of liberalisation.

A **cut in the volume of subsidised EU exports** would tend, other things being equal, to result in an increase (probably relatively small) in world prices. This would mean higher export revenues for net exporters, and larger import bills for importers. As such, the effects would be similar to those of liberalisation, but much less marked. This is because the level of world production is expected to be much higher following simply a cut in the EU's subsidised exports than it would be as a result of full EU trade liberalisation.

Measures that are aimed at **restricting EU production** (such as set-asides and dairy quotas) will not have any direct external effects. Only if there are knock-on effects on, for example, exports or the volume of permitted imports (neither of which is inevitable) will there be third-party effects.

Similarly, a **cut in administered EU prices** would not affect importing States directly, but it could have an impact on exporters. To the extent that it affects those products for which some, preferred, exporters have access to the European market and receive EU prices, it will result in a fall in the revenue generated by this access. Hence, for example, a fall in administrative prices for beef or sugar would result in a net loss for the Sugar and Beef Protocol countries. Their existing quota of exports would generate less foreign exchange and they would have no opportunity to offset this by an increase in the volume of exports.

The special effects on the ACP as preference beneficiaries

The combination of EU agricultural protectionism and trade preferences has had three types of

Table 8. Implications of CAP reform for the chain of effect

Type of reform	Implications for:	
	exporters	importers
Liberalisation of access to EU market	Increased world demand But ? lower EU prices: • shift from inefficient preferred to efficient non-preferred suppliers	Higher import prices
Cut in subsidised EU exports	Higher export prices	Higher import prices
Restriction of EU production	No direct effect (unless exports affected)	
Cut in administered EU prices	Lower prices for preferred exporters without offsetting volume increase	No effect

effect that vary between ACP States in their relative and absolute importance.

❖ World prices for many temperate agricultural products have been artificially depressed. This has been particularly marked in the case of wheat, other cereals, red meat, dairy products and sugar. In consequence, imports of these products have been cheaper than they would have been under a more liberal trade regime, and exports of these items have been financially less attractive than would otherwise have been the case.

❖ World prices have been more volatile than would have been the case had a large section of world producers and consumers not been insulated from market forces. In consequence, the burden of adjusting to supply shocks (such as poor harvests) has been borne disproportionately by developing countries, many of which do not have the resources effectively to protect their producers and consumers from world market forces.

❖ The combination of artificially high prices in the ACP's main market, the EU, and trade preferences has made the export of some items particularly attractive for the countries of the region. These are sugar and beef covered by the relevant Lomé Protocols, together with horticulture and floriculture.

These three sets of forces will have tended to make the cost of importing basic staples into the region more attractive financially than is justified by the underlying costs of production in the rest of the world, and to have made exporting horti-culture/ sugar/beef more attractive than would otherwise have been the case. These pressures may have contributed to the present pattern of production and supply in the region by reducing the incentive to supply staples from within the region and increasing the incentive to use region-al agricultural resources for export purposes.

Although the immediate effects of the Uruguay Round and CAP reform for world cereal availability and prices may be limited, a plausible case can be made that it would be prudent for the ACP to start planning now for a more food insecure future. This is because:

❖ the heavy import dependence of many ACP States is already a source of great vulnerability to changes elsewhere (as the high world prices of 1996 illustrated);

❖ further change to OECD agriculture is on the cards for early next century;

❖ there may be more profound short-term changes affecting the intra-sectoral terms of trade for ACP agriculture that need to be taken into account.

The thread of the argument is that: the principal achievement of the Uruguay Round has been to start the process of applying normal GATT disciplines to agriculture but at the cost of limited change in the short term; the changes that will be made may have disproportionate effects on the ACP because of the particular dependence of many group members on wheat imports and the EU as a supplier; the impact of liberalisation affecting ACP imports may be reinforced by the effects of liberalisation on its exports; and that the potential adverse effects of a rundown in publicly managed stocks in OECD States may be greater for ACP States than for other regions both because of its dependence on food aid and because its fragile balance-of-payments position makes its ill-placed to cope with world price instability.

The Stimulus of EU Enlargement

The EU is expected to enlarge both its geographical area and its range of competences in the coming years. Both will have indirect effects on the traditional EU–ACP relationship. It is difficult, and probably not terribly helpful, to attempt a precise identification of these effects, but the general trends may be sketched.

The geographical extension of Europe to include the countries of Central and Eastern Europe as well as some Baltic States will have both positive and negative effects on trade with the ACP and, probably, negative effects on trade policy formation. The adoption by these new entrants of the the EU's Common Commercial Policy will give the ACP the same advantages *vis-à-vis* their competitors in the markets of the new entrants that they have in the existing fifteen Member States. Since the ACP produce a significant number of 'exotic' commodities, it is entirely possible that they will see a measurable growth in demand for their exports. At the same time, there could be some offsetting competition on the market of the 15 from the products of the new entrants. However, while this may be a significant problem for many developing countries it would not appear to pose a particularly serious challenge for the ACP, given the commodity composition of their exports. Had the ACP been more successful in diversifying into manufactures than they have been, then the danger of increased competition with the new entrants would be greater.

The most likely source of negative effects on the ACP is via the influence of the new entrants on trade policy. The political centre of gravity of Europe will shift.

Not only may the new entrants have a different, and possibly more protectionist, attitude towards trade policy than the existing 15, but also the problems of adjustment thrown up by enlargement may well provoke a change in attitudes in the existing Member States. This could rebound to the benefit of the ACP, but this is probably unlikely. The reason for the possible favourable reaction is that preferences are the reciprocal of protectionism. If protectionism increases, then the value of derogations from it is greater for the preference beneficiaries. Unfortunately, the shift in emphasis in trade policy away from tariffs and quotas as the principal form of protection probably means that the ACP may not see an increase in their bene-

fits as a result of greater protectionism. The new forms of protection, if they occur, could well take novel forms (such as the continued extension of anti-dumping actions or the use of voluntary export restraints). The provisions of the Lomé Convention would not exempt the ACP from such action. In this sense, the need to move beyond Lomé in any successor arrangement to deal with the new trade agenda, as well as the old, is important.

The effect on the ACP of policy change may be much wider than this. It could affect elements of Lomé such as the aid programme. This is because if the EU adopts a more extensive form of co-operation in foreign and defence policy it may have less need for a common aid policy. It is in this sense that functional, as opposed to geographical, enlargement of the EU may affect the Lomé relationship.

The rationale for a Union-level aid programme is not immediately obvious. Under the Maastricht Treaty, aid was identified as an area in which there were no necessary Union functions under the principle of subsidiarity. The Treaty merely recognised the fact that national- and Union-level aid programmes co-exist side by side. Since the Union-level programme is financed from the contributions of the Member States (i.e. from the total aid allocations of the members), and does not yet focus exclusively on areas of aid policy that are handled more appropriately at Union than at national level, it is not easy to understand without the benefit of history exactly why a Union-level programme exists.

The principal reasons why Union-level aid policies exist are partly burden-sharing (particularly in the early years, when France's partners agreed to an EEC aid programme to its (former) colonies), and partly as a substitute foreign policy. As explained earlier in Part 1, the European Commission has used some skill to develop a quasi foreign policy using trade preferences and aid as its principal tools.

If the Union develops genuine foreign and defence policies, then the need for this substitute will disappear. Although this would not necessarily mean a downgrading of the ACP, there is a significant danger that this would happen. This is because the ACP's position in Europe's quasi foreign policy hierarchy is higher than its current economic and strategic importance to Europe would justify. Any formulation of a new policy, therefore, would run the risk of the ACP being positioned at a point appropriate to their current importance to the EU, not their importance of a quarter century ago.

Part 2

Terms of a REPA

The EU's proposed REPAs suggest that it has as its medium-term objective the expansion of the set of FTAs that occupy the second layer in the pyramid of privilege (see Figure 1). If bilateral and plurilateral FTAs do form an important part of the EU's vision of the future, it is important that their potential economic effects be well understood. This part of the report provides an introduction to the effects of different types of stylised FTA which will serve as a benchmark against which to judge actual agreements. To assist this process, the theoretical section is followed by a review of two of the EU's recent FTAs: the one with Morocco that has been completed and the one with South Africa which, while still under negotiation, is sufficiently well-known to permit conclusions to be drawn on the EU's preferences in such accords.

The Economic Effects of an FTA
A simple Vinerian model

The decrease in tariffs[6] associated with the FTA would benefit the developing partner countries by lowering prices to consumers and by improving the allocation of resources. The decrease in import prices as a result of the abolition of tariffs against imports from the EU would increase the size of the consumers' surplus. In the Vinerian model of perfectly elastic supply curves this will come about through:

❖ the transfer of tariff revenue previously levied on imports from the EU from the government to consumers;

❖ the replacement of less efficient domestic producers of importables, who were previously able to remain in production only as a result of import protection, by lower-priced imports from the EU.

This is illustrated in Figure 2. The gain in the consumers' surplus from the loss of tariff revenue is simply an internal transfer (unless value judgements are made regarding the superiority of consumers' expenditure over government expenditure). By contrast, the replacement of some domestic production by increased imports from the EU is an efficiency gain, since resources are released from less productive activities to (potentially) more productive activities, although it should be noted that this re-allocation of resources will involve adjustment costs.

These gains would be limited, and could be completely offset, by the fact that under a bilateral FTA the partner would only be liberalising trade with the EU, and tariffs would remain on imports from the rest of the world (RW). For those products in which the EU is not the least-cost source of supply, an FTA can therefore divert imports from a more efficient source of supply (RW) to a less efficient source of supply (EU). This is illustrated in Figure 3. This will result in a decrease in production and welfare in RW and gains to consumers in the partner country and EU exporters. The gains to consumers in the developing partner will result from the decrease in import prices. But part of this increase in the consumers' surplus will simply be an internal transfer of import revenue from the government to consumers, and only a relatively small part will represent the efficiency gains arising from the displacement of less efficient (than EU) domestic producers. Part of

---

6   In the following discussion, 'tariffs' will be used as a shorthand description for all border restrictions which are removed by the FTA.

Figure 2 Perfectly elastic supply from RW and EU – trade creation

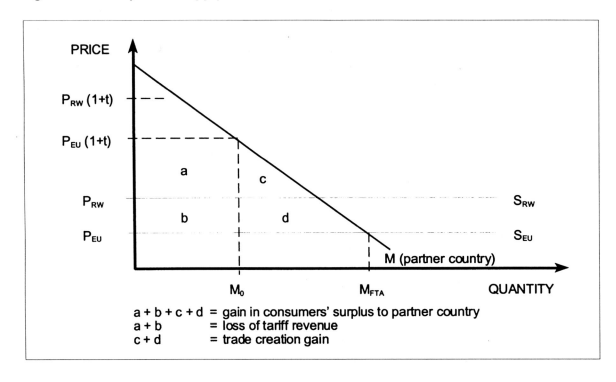

a + b + c + d = gain in consumers' surplus to partner country
a + b = loss of tariff revenue
c + d = trade creation gain

Figure 3 Perfectly elastic supply from RW and EU – trade diversion

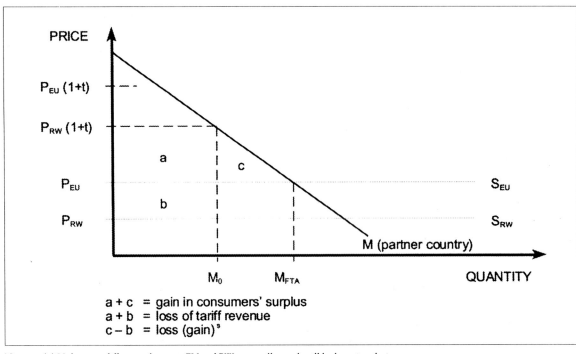

a + c = gain in consumers' surplus
a + b = loss of tariff revenue
c − b = loss (gain) [a]

Note: (a) Unless cost differences between EU and RW are small, area b will be large in relation to c.

the loss of tariff revenue will also be redistributed to EU exporters, since they are a higher-cost source of imports than RW. Unless the excess of EU over RW f.o.b. prices is very small, the resource *costs* of the FTA for the developing partner (equal to the previous volume of imports from the EU multiplied by the excess of EU prices over RW prices) could be greater than the efficiency *gain* (the 'triangle' of the net increase in the consumers' surplus) from lower import prices.

The balance between the trade creation and trade diversion effects and the welfare effects of an FTA will vary according to the circumstances of the case, and its determination is an empirical question. The magnitude of both effects will be smaller, the smaller the initial share of imports from the EU in developing partner countries' total dutiable imports.

❖ The *trade creation* effects will depend on the extent to which imports from the EU are substitutes for developing partner country production.

❖ The *trade diversion* effects will depend on the extent to which imports from the EU are substitutes for imports from RW, and the extent to which EU (pre-tariff) prices exceed RW (pre-tariff) prices.

The effects of upward-sloping curves of EU and RW exports

This simple model captures the basic effects of increased developing partner imports from the EU as a result of an FTA, but it relies on the simplifying assumption of perfectly elastic supply curves for imports, with the implication that the developing partners import particular products from either the EU or RW, but not both. If we assume, instead, that developing partner imports from RW are in perfectly elastic supply (being small markets relative to the USA, etc.) but that the supply of imports from the EU is less than perfectly elastic (given the distance between the two markets) then shifts within-FTA terms of trade produce additional effects. These are illustrated in Figure 4.

Figure 4 Less than perfectly elastic supply from EU, perfectly elastic supply from RW

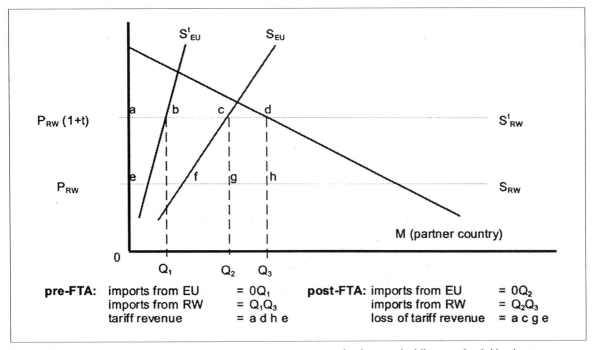

pre-FTA: imports from EU = $0Q_1$
imports from RW = Q_1Q_3
tariff revenue = a d h e

post-FTA: imports from EU = $0Q_2$
imports from RW = Q_2Q_3
loss of tariff revenue = a c g e

Note: Import price is unchanged, so no trade creation; partner country terms of trade worsen by full extent of trade liberalisation.

If it is assumed that developing partners import both from the EU and from RW, the effect of the FTA is different, and tends to increase the gains for the EU relative to partner countries. It shifts the EU's supply curve of exports to developing partners outwards by the extent of the abolition of tariffs but, because RW's supply curve is perfectly elastic and developing partners continue to import from RW after the FTA, the price of imports within the developing partner countries remains unchanged. Hence, the EU gains:

❖ from the substitution of RW goods by tariff-free EU goods (but the substitution is incomplete because of EU's rising supply curves);

❖ and from capturing the whole of the tariff revenue on this increased volume of imports.

There are no trade creation effects and developing partners' within-FTA terms of trade deteriorate by the full amount of the tariff liberalisation.

The magnitude of these effects will depend upon:

❖ the initial share of the EU in total developing partner dutiable imports;

❖ the size of the tariff;

❖ and the price elasticity of demand for imports.

For example, it is theoretically possible that a high initial tariff and large EU import share, combined with a low price elasticity of demand for imports, could shift the EU's export supply curve outwards to such an extent that the import price falls below RW's supply price. The FTA would then generate trade creation gains without trade diversion losses, and under strong assumptions these could outweigh the tariff revenue loss. This, however, is implausible in a world of imperfect competition, and we would therefore expect EU exporters to limit the volume of exports to developing partners to a revenue maximising level (which will depend on the developing part-

ners' price elasticity of demand for imports from the EU) which will capture at least some of the gains from preferential treatment.

Differences in transport and transaction costs may also be relevant to an EU–developing partner FTA (Bhagwati and Panagariya, 1996). If these costs are substantially lower for the USA than for the EU, but other costs are identical for these two suppliers, then under the initial non-discriminatory tariff, the marginal cost of imports from the EU is higher than from the USA. Since the EU has the higher price elasticity of supply, an FTA with the EU would be preferable to one with the USA, contrary to the view that high transport costs make groupings of distant motives economically inefficient (Wonnacott and Lutz, 1989).

Dynamic gains

Trade creation and trade diversion have only once-and-for-all effects on the *level* of national income and do not alter the *trend* rate of growth of the economy. Empirical studies of preferential trade arrangements emphasise gains from using unexploited economies of scale and increased competition, raising the growth of productivity. Since an FTA would provide the same access to the EU market as Lomé preferences, there would not appear to be any opportunity for further gains through scale economies in relation to partner country exports.

Liberalising trade with the EU may, however, create a more competitive domestic environment (if import prices fall), reducing oligopolistic pricing practices and excessive diversification of production with consequent high costs of production (especially in the small partner country economies) and increasing the range and quality of products available to producers and consumers. If the FTA enables producers to purchase inputs from the EU at world prices rather than tariff-distorted prices, then this may encourage domestic investment and the diversification of exports and import substitutes and raise both the growth and stability of net foreign exchange earnings.

These effects may be reinforced if the FTA can act as an 'anchor' for general trade liberalisation. Unilateral trade liberalisation may have only a limited success in stimulating the growth of an economy if commercial decision takers consider that the programme of import liberalisation may be reversed in the future. An FTA, however, is legally binding and import liberalisation could be reversed only if the country withdrew from the arrangement – a much more serious step. An FTA may therefore provide external validity to a trade liberalisation programme and maximise the gains from such a policy.

The strength of this effect will be affected by the proportion of the developing partner's trade that occurs under the FTA. If the EU is a minor trade partner then, unless there is substantial trade diversion, the anchor may be perceived as somewhat fragile.

Foreign investment

One of the most important potential benefits from an FTA between developed and developing countries is in attracting flows of foreign direct investment (FDI) into the developing countries. FDI is important not so much for bringing capital as for transferring knowledge about what to produce, how to produce, how to control, finance and manage an enterprise, co-ordinate production and suppliers, continuously improve productivity and quality control, access markets, etc. Much of this knowledge is proprietary to the enterprise and cannot be purchased, or can only be imperfectly acquired through arm's-length contracts.

Foreign production is the strategic response of firms to changes in relative competitiveness and locational advantages. Since reciprocal preferences alter relative prices of goods in different locations, we can expect preferences to influence flows of FDI. An FTA may induce firms in RW to offset the trade diversion effects of the agreement by locating production in developing partner countries, and this is termed *investment creation*. Trade creation requires the reorganisa-

tion of production within the FTA, and EU firms may decide to locate production in developing partner countries to take advantage of other locational advantages, both to serve the partner country market and for export to the EU and RW. This is termed *investment diversion*.

The scale of these potential effects will depend upon a range of factors. Individual countries in the region will probably provide too small a domestic market to attract FDI serving the home market. Hence the effectiveness of the FTA attracting import substituting investment will depend upon the degree of actual free trade between the countries of the region and the cost and availability of transport. FDI for export markets will depend upon the costs of locating in partner countries relative to other locations and the rules of origin governing preferential access to the EU and US markets.

Diffusion of knowledge and technology will depend, among other things, on the production activities of the foreign investors (whether they are an export platform, import substituting, resource-based, or in the service sector) and their forms of investment (wholly-owned affiliates, joint ventures, etc.). Surveys of existing FDI may provide some indication of these factors.

Contents of the agreement

It is often remarked of international trade agreements that the 'devil is in the detail', and this is certainly true of FTAs. Of the many issues involved, some in particular can be emphasised. First, given the strengthening of WTO procedures, will the content of the agreement be compatible with WTO rules, especially regarding a narrow interpretation of Article XXIV? Will the agreement seek to go beyond WTO rules and deepen economic relations, for example concerning EU competition rules, regulations governing standards, health and safety, guarantees of national treatment for foreign investors, rights of natural persons (particularly affecting the provision of services), trade-related investment measures (TRIMs) and intellectual property rights? Are the rules of origin likely to assist or inhibit partner countries in benefiting from the agreement, and will they encourage or retard regional integration? What trade- and investment-related financial and technical co-operation provisions will be included in the agreement, and are these likely to enhance significantly the benefits obtained from the agreement?

Transitional arrangements are also important since they provide important 'signals' governing the response of economic agents and influence the long-term effects of the agreement. If duties are eliminated over a 12-year schedule which end-weights reductions in tariffs on high-tariff items, for example, this may ease the adjustment problems in terms of reductions in government import revenues and protection for the least competitive sectors of the economy. But the schedule also increases effective rates of protection when a key element of structural adjustment programmes is to reduce effective protection by 'concertina' reductions in tariffs (i.e. decreasing high-tariff items by a greater proportion than low-tariff items).

Hub-and-spoke effects

The preceding analysis of the general static and dynamic effects of an FTA between the EU and a developing country did not take into account any additional effects that might arise from the Commission's current proposals for the EU to conclude separate agreements, with differing content, with a number of ACP sub-regions. It also abstracted from the wider picture in which the EU has already concluded 27 reciprocal trade agreements with other countries, notably in Central and Eastern Europe and the Mediterranean, as well as with the European Free Trade Association (EFTA) countries.

The 'common denominator' in all of these agreements is the EU, which – on the analogy of airline routing systems – becomes an EU–EFTA bloc 'hub', with 'spokes' radiating out via bilateral agreements to countries and groups of countries on the spokes. Economic analysis has suggested that, by comparison with an overall FTA, the collective increase in incomes of such hub-and-spoke arrangements is lower, the gains from this lower level of collective income are more concentrated in the hub (the EU), and the agreements may damage potential spoke–spoke trade (intra-Caribbean/Latin American regional trade, intra-ACP country trade, Eastern Europe and the Mediterranean countries).

These effects can best be appreciated by comparing the decisions facing exporters and investors in the EU and developing partners under Lomé with those that would apply under an FTA. Under the present arrangements, each ACP country maintains its own border restrictions and does not discriminate between imports from the EU and other non-regional suppliers. An EU producer has therefore to decide between exporting to the developing partner's market or jumping over the border restrictions and servicing the partner's local or regional market via import-substituting FDI. These decisions will depend solely on:

❖ the transaction costs of exporting versus the costs of producing in the partner country;

❖ the size of the market.

Developing partner exporters – local, regional, or EU companies based in partner countries – can 'cumulate origin'. That is, they can use imports from the EU, other ACP countries and local resources in any combination to fulfil the minimum-processing and value-added criteria of the Lomé rules of origin in order to qualify for preferential treatment by the EU. This cumulation rule therefore potentially encourages intra-ACP trade as well as ACP–EU trade. At the same time, third countries can still supply the developing partner market, provided the prices of their intermediate products are sufficiently lower than EU prices to more than offset the EU duty on the final product.

With separate FTAs for each ACP sub-region, the product coverage, transitional arrangements, rules of origin and other details of the agreements can be expected to differ. Countries will wish to maintain the integrity of their border restrictions against other countries, so the transactions costs of trade, including regional trade, will rise. As a result, producers (EU and non-EU alike) will have an increased incentive when deciding how best to service the ACP market of economies of scale and lower transactions costs to locate in the EU rather than an ACP country. Since only the EU has preferential access (guaranteed by treaty) to all of the ACP countries which have concluded co-operation and partnership agreements, it will tend to be a more attractive location than any one of the sub-regions.

'The hub's special advantages [over the spokes] in trade . . . [translate] into an advantage in attracting investment' (Wonnacott, 1996, p. 246). This investment disadvantage of the ACP countries could become cumulative. These hub-and-spoke costs can be reduced, though not eliminated, by minimising the variations in the content, including rules of origin, of the EU's agreements both with developing partners and with all groups with which a partner has, or envisages having, significant trade relations.

The Agreement with Morocco

The EU's FTAs with the non-EU Mediterranean countries are the only example of such agreements with developing countries; as discussed in Part 1, they have become an increasingly important focus of attention for EU development co-operation. Within the Euro–Med agreements can be found elements of the EU negotiating mandate for the development of partnership agreements with the ACP concerning, for example, the EU's interpretation of WTO compatibility (product coverage and transition period), the promotion of competition policy, rights of establishment, liberalisation of current account transactions, financial co-operation and institutional arrangements.

Of the two Euro–Med FTAs so far concluded, the agreement with Morocco has been selected because of Morocco's broad similarity with a number of ACP countries; its *per capita* GNP is just below that of Jamaica and agriculture is of central importance to the economy, accounting for 22 per cent of GDP, 3 per cent of employment and 23 per cent of exports to the EU. Also, given the EU's undoubted concern over the need to increase the growth of output and employment and decrease the gap in standards of living between the Mediterranean countries and the EU in order to increase political stability and reduce migratory pressures on the EU, we could expect the agreement with Morocco to be as generous as possible within the limits set by the internal constraints of the EU.

The major elements to the agreement are:

❖ political dialogue and institutional provisions;

❖ the free movement of goods;

❖ the right of establishment and supply of services;

❖ movements of capital;

❖ competition policy;

❖ other economic provisions (including dumping and the safeguard clause, arbitration and the rules of origin);

❖ financial co-operation.

Political dialogue

Political dialogue is achieved through an Association Council (at ministerial level) and an Association Committee (at senior official level, with representatives of Morocco, the Council Presidency and the Commission). The Association Committee is essentially responsible for the implementation of the Agreement and has powers provided for in the Agreement or which can be delegated to it by the Association Council. Interestingly, there is no reference in the agreement to administrative arrangements for co-ordinating action on a Mediterranean-wide basis despite the EU's objective of establishing a Euro–Med FTA; the ACP should ensure that adequate arrangements are put in place to organise and co-ordinate action to encourage not only *intra*-regional trade but also *inter*-regional trade, particularly in sub-Saharan Africa.

Free movement of goods

The free trade area is to be established over a 12-year transitional period starting from the entry into force of the agreement.

Under the terms of the 1976 Co-operation Agreement Morocco already obtained duty-free access for industrial goods exported to the EU (with the exception of those referred to in Annex II of the Treaty of Rome, covering products of the European Coal and Steel Community) and concessions on agricultural products (subject to restrictions of the CAP), and these are simply continued on an indefinite basis in the FTA.

Imports from the EU are subject to a complex system of trade liberalisation. Industrial products are covered by four different schedules of tariff reductions:

❖ products subject to immediate tariff reductions (with some restrictions, including tariff quotas on some processed agricultural products);

❖ products subject to a three-year transition, with a 75 per cent reduction in tariffs in year one;

❖ products subject to a 12-year transition, starting in year three;

❖ products on which tariffs are abolished in year one and minimum import prices abolished in year three.

The tariff schedules are completed with a list of products exempt from tariff reductions, but where import quotas must be abolished (although in some cases this takes place only at the end of the 12-year transitional period).

The general pattern of liberalisation of imports of industrial products from the EU is that low tariffs on imports of intermediate products used in production and capital goods are abolished early on in the 12-year period, and imports of consumer goods subject to high tariffs are liberalised towards the end of the transitional period.

Imports of agricultural products from the EU which compete with production in Morocco are subject to customs duties which mirror those of the CAP (e.g. 168 per cent on 'beet sugar other than for refining' and 215 per cent on various animal and vegetable fats, and tariff quotas). There is an agreement to 'gradually implement greater liberalisation of reciprocal trade in agricultural and fisheries products' and an assessment of the situation is scheduled for 1 January 2000, but no firm commitments are made.

Lessons for the ACP

The phasing over time of the removal of import restrictions on EU products which Morocco successfully negotiated required a major effort. For example, just two of the six Annexes detailing the schedules of import liberalisation covered no fewer than 1,700 entries. The ACP countries will have to carry out a similar exercise, but with the even more formidable task of producing an agreed list not just for one country but for all of the countries covered by the REPAs.

The pattern of import liberalisation on industrial goods, although ostensibly easing the adjustment to free trade with the EU, may have adverse economic consequences.

There are two important reasons for this pattern of trade liberalisation. First, around 18 per cent of government revenues come from import duties, and most of the revenues from imports from the EU come from imports of consumer goods. Liberalising these goods last of all will provide time for a restructuring of sources of government revenues. Second, this pattern of liberalisation seeks to assist local firms adjusting to free trade with the EU in two ways. First, there is a gradual, rather than a rapid, reduction in nominal levels of protection by tariffs on goods which will have to compete eventually with imports from the EU. Second, and more problematically, local firms will be able (at least for the first part of the transitional period) to purchase imports of investment goods and intermediate products from the EU at lower prices while still being able to sell their output in the domestic market at tariff-inflated prices. This will raise profit margins on these protected goods and *potentially* enable firms to engage in investment and reorganisation to raise levels of productivity. The increased profit levels are, however, obtained at the expense of government import revenues and of consumers, who continue to have to pay higher tariff-inflated prices. This constitutes a welfare loss.

The key word is *potentially*, as this pattern of trade liberalisation is not guaranteed to produce adjustment. The enhanced level of profits on these goods may lead to inefficient investment in the sense that increased production induced by higher levels of profitability may be unable to compete in free trade with EU goods. Also, the increase in effective protection of domestic industries during the first part of the implementation period may – especially given that the implementation of the adjustment process is over a 12-year period – induce complacency and insufficient adjustment by existing firms.

It is precisely for this reason that World Bank structural adjustment programmes emphasise the importance of 'concertina' reductions in tariffs, under which high tariffs are reduced by larger absolute amounts than low tariffs. This reduces not only the average level of protection but also the deviation of tariffs around the average, thus reducing effective levels of protection and exerting pressure for increased efficiency in the allocation of resources. Over half Morocco's imports come from the EU and so the FTA substantially undermines Morocco's structural adjustment agreement with the World Bank, despite the EU's insistence, at various points in the agreement (for example, Article 76), on the importance of both parties working with the international financial institutions.

The combination of confusing messages

regarding the necessary direction of structural adjustment and the lack of immediate benefits to consumers may weaken support for the FTA and the credibility of the government's commitment to the agreement. The danger then is that a vicious circle may be set in motion in which pressures emerge for resistance to continued opening of the market either with the EU or to imports in general.

The ACP may, therefore, wish to consider alternative strategies of liberalisation. One would be to synchronise the transitional period for the implementation of the REPA with general structural adjustment and trade liberalisation strategies. Alternatively, if it is thought desirable to follow Morocco's pattern for liberalising imports from the EU, the ACP countries could borrow from the experience of the newly industrialised countries and make protection conditional on meeting performance criteria, with penalties for firms which fail to do so.

From the point of view of the efficient allocation of resources, the most desirable method of adjustment to free trade with the EU would be one in which levels of effective protection are reduced as quickly as practicable and support for uncompetitive industries is concentrated on financial and technical assistance, subject to constraints which seek to limit moral hazard (false claims by firms) and adverse selection (problems of distinguishing between firms that are potentially competitive under free trade and those which are not).

In the case of agricultural products, the objectives of the EU are quite clearly stated in Protocol 1, Article: 2.5:

❖ the aim of the specific arrangements established by this Article shall be to preserve the level of Morocco's traditional exports to the Community and to avoid disturbing Community markets.

It is not surprising, therefore, that little will change as far as Morocco's access to the EU for agricultural exports is concerned. There are limited improvements in access for specific products through an expansion of tariff quotas and the reduction or elimination of tariffs for specific quotas. It should be noted that these were very often obtained only after lengthy and acrimonious negotiations. Even here, preferential treatment for sensitive products ceases as soon as EU produce comes to the market. Minimum import prices have been set so high above the internal EU prices that Morocco is effectively excluded from the market. The conclusion of a recent World Bank study 'Growing Faster, Finding Jobs' (World Bank, 1996) 'that the prospects for further growth of agricultural exports to the EU appear very limited' does not seem to be overstating the case.

In none of the EU's agreements has trade in agricultural products been fully liberalised, and this implies that the ACP can expect, at best, to retain their existing market access for CAP products and indeed may have to fight hard to retain existing levels of access for Protocol products (sugar, beef, rice and bananas). It seems unlikely that they will be able to obtain any significant additional concessions during the negotiation of REPAs.

Right of establishment and supply of services

The agreement provides for increasing trade and investment through agreements on the right of establishment of firms in each other's territories and the liberalisation of the provision of services by one party's firms to consumers of services in the other, although no timetable is laid down for the achievement of this objective. The Association Council is simply required to make recommendations for achieving these objectives, with the proviso that it will, *inter alia*, take account of the obligations of each party under the General Agreement on Trade in Services (GATS). The Association Council is also required to make the first assessment of the achievement of these objectives not later than five years after the Agreement comes into force. It is also required, as one of its first priorities, to examine the international maritime transport sector, with a view to making appropriate recommendations for liberalisation measures.

The lack of precision in the section covering rights of establishment and services undoubtedly reflects the sensitivity of issues involving EU direct investment in Morocco (right of establishment) and the free movement of persons into the EU (associated with the supply of services). The ACP countries will similarly have to decide policy in these areas. Lack of precision regarding rights of establishment may deter EU direct investment which would otherwise have been attracted to the ACP countries by a REPA. Also, the ACP will have to formulate joint policies regarding the role of foreign enterprises in significantly improving the supply and quality of key services necessary to modernise the economy (for example, telecommunications and financial services). They will also have to decide jointly whether these policy objectives can best be achieved within an FTA with the EU (the Eastern European countries, for example, have granted free entry and national treatment to EU firms, with transitional periods for a limited number of sectors and activities), or whether they could obtain a better supply of these key services by making binding obligations within the GATS and potentially opening up the supply of these services to international competition, rather than giving preferential access to EU enterprises.

Movements of capital

More generally, it is usually accepted that trade and investment by multinational companies are complementary instruments of international production and marketing and, as a result, developing countries are increasingly advised to pursue a policy of 'modal neutrality'. This implies that they should pursue equality of policy treatment irrespective of the *means* by which producers decide to supply and service a market. According to this view, import liberalisation with the EU should be matched by investment liberalisation for EU firms locating in ACP countries.

Unrestricted national treatment, however, implies a large loss of national sovereignty and a weakening of bargaining power for host countries in their relationships with multinational companies. Investment agreements therefore frequently contain exceptions and limitations, although it should be noted that these restrictions must be WTO-compatible. This applies particularly to the TRIMs Agreement which prohibits trade (in goods only) related measures which are in violation of Article III (national treatment obligations) and Article XI (elimination of qualitative restrictions). These exceptions and limitations can take the form of a 'negative list', with national treatment applying *unless* a stipulation is made to the contrary (for example, in the North American Free Trade Agreement (NAFTA)). This is potentially the most liberal type of such an arrangement. The alternative is a 'positive list', stating the activities where commitments apply (for example the GATS agreements), with the explicit understanding that, unless listed, national treatment does *not* apply.

Arrangements such as these would assist the ACP to achieve the objective in their negotiating mandate of giving 'high priority to attracting both local and foreign direct investment, particularly of European origin' (ACP Negotiating Mandate/28/028/98 Ref.2.Neg.para.68). While deepening relations with the EU in ways which would be conducive to FDI would be potentially beneficial to the ACP countries, it is essential that this is achieved in ways which do not deter investment from non-EU industrialised countries and from other ACP countries.

The Agreements covering convertibility and capital controls are wide-ranging and, although they do not go beyond GATT and IMF provisions on temporary restrictions, in the case of balance-of-payments difficulties they require that the Community or Morocco, as the case may be, must inform the other party forthwith (of such measures) and 'shall submit to it as soon as possible a timetable for the elimination of the measures concerned' (Article 35).

Competition policy, State aid and procurement

One feature of the FTA that may be of particular interest to the ACP is that Morocco is required to adopt the competition rules of the EU. Particular areas mentioned are collusive behaviour, abuse of dominant position and competition-distorting State aids, insofar as they affect trade between the EU and Morocco. For, example Article 36.1 (c) States that among the things which are incompatible with the functioning of the agreement in so far as they may affect trade between the Community and Morocco is:

❖ any State aid which distorts or threatens to distort competition by favouring certain undertakings or the production of certain goods, with the exception of cases in which a derogation is allowed under the Treaty establishing the European Coal and Steel Community.

Note that the only exceptions are for EU practices, and that the operations of the CAP are not even regarded as anti-competitive.

For the purposes of assessing the application of the provisions of paragraph 1 (c) during the first five years after the entry into force of the Agreement, Morocco is to be regarded as if it were a disadvantaged region of the Community, as described in Article 92(3)(a) of the Treaty of Rome. Morocco may also, exceptionally, as regards ECSC steel products, grant State aid for restructuring purposes, provided that this leads to the viability of the recipient firms under normal market conditions at the end of the restructuring period, is strictly limited to what is absolutely necessary and is linked to a comprehensive plan for rationalising capacity in Morocco.

With regard to State monopolies, Article 37 states that:

❖ both Parties shall progressively adjust… any State monopolies of a commercial character so as to ensure that, by the end of the fifth year following the entry into force of this agreement, no discrimination regarding the conditions under which goods are procured and marketed exists between nationals of the member States and of Morocco. The Association Committee will be informed about the measures adopted to implement this objective.

In order to ensure the enforcement of competition policy and subsidy rules the Association Council is required to adopt rules to enforce these disciplines within five years of the entry into force of the Agreement.

The EU negotiating mandate appears to be less coercive with respect to the use of competition policy, and simply offers to assist the ACP in this area. This is an offer which the ACP need to consider seriously, since there are potentially significant advantages in the proposal. First, the potential economic benefits from a REPA depend on the price of imports from the EU falling by the amount of the tariffs (and tariff equivalent of the non-tariff barriers) removed by the FTA. If markets are uncompetitive because of the dominant position of EU or ACP firms, then the REPA will simply transfer the loss of government revenue to these dominant firms. Second, it is questionable whether the liberalisation of an investment regime can be effective without an effective policy on competition to ensure that, as far as possible, markets are contestable. Multinational companies, in particular, derive an important part of their competitive position from *firm-specific* advantages, such as knowledge and intellectual property rights (and the Agreement on Trade-Related Aspects of Intellectual Property Rights (TRIPs) has strengthened their position). This knowledge, in combination with internalisation advantages, generally increases the market power of multinationals, especially in small developing countries with close links with only one or two industrialised countries. Effective implementation of EU competition policy (a difficult task, admittedly) would provide EU investors with a familiar economic environment in which to operate, while at the same time

controlling any abuse of market power. More generally, drawing on the accumulated experience and knowledge of the EU in this field should prevent some ACP countries trying to develop their own policies in this difficult area of policy making. The important *caveat* to this proposal is that EU competition policy will probably have to be adapted to the different economic conditions in the ACP countries (including the small size of the domestic market) and the ability of ACP countries effectively to enforce the policy.

In common with its other FTAs, the EU requires 'suitable and effective protection of intellectual, industrial and commercial property rights, in line was the highest international standards', together with effective means of enforcing such rights, and the implementation of this is to be regularly assessed by both parties. This simply reinforces the requirements of the TRIPs agreement and does not add any additional requirements. The ACP could, however, use a REPA to obtain additional assistance, both in implementing the agreement and in using the safeguards it gives to intellectual property rights, to stimulate the transfer of technology to ACP countries.

The use by Morocco of Community technical rules and European standards for industrial and agri-food products and certification procedures is 'to be promoted' and, 'when the circumstances are right', agreements are to be concluded for the mutual recognition of certification. These rules and standards are increasingly becoming important non-tariff barriers to trade, and the ACP could usefully utilise a REPA to provide clear commitments from the EU in the field.

Finally, under Article 41, the aim is for a reciprocal and gradual liberalisation of public procurement contracts.

Dumping and safeguard clauses

Despite the requirement that Morocco adopt the EU's competition rules, the agreement also allows for the use of countervailing duties if 'dumping' takes place in trade within the meaning of Article VI of the GATT. This is a clear inconsistency in the agreement, since the only valid reasons for using anti-dumping actions should be predatory pricing and other related actions proscribed by competition rules. The European Economic Area (EEA) agreement, for example, included EU competition rules and excluded anti-dumping actions. The only reason for including both is if the EU envisaged going beyond the legitimate purposes of anti-dumping actions and using the notoriously weak WTO disciplines in this area as a non-tariff barrier to trade. If the ACP agree to implement EU competition policy, they should, therefore, also insist that anti-dumping processes are excluded and that both parties waive their rights under Article VI of the GATT.

Article 25 is the safeguard clause, and states that:
> Where any product is being imported in such increased quantities and under such conditions as to cause or threaten to cause:
>
> ❖ serious injury to domestic producers of like or directly competitive products in the territory of one of the contracting parties,
> ❖ serious disturbances in any sector of the economy or difficulties which could bring about serious deterioration in the economic situation of a region,
>
> the Community or Morocco may take appropriate measures under the conditions and in accordance with the procedures laid down in Article 27.

This safeguard clause is more restrictive than that in Lomé IV (Article 177) which refers to 'result in', not 'threaten to cause', serious disturbances. Also, Lomé only refers to a 'sector of the economy' of the Community and not also to 'serious injury to domestic producers of like or directly competitive products'. The ACP countries need to ensure that the REPAs do not 'harmonise' any safeguard clause (if one is included) on their more restrictive version.

During the 12-year transitional period Morocco may also take, under Article 14, exceptional measures of limited duration which derogate from the schedule of reductions in customs duties under Article 11, in the form of an increase or reintroduction of customs duties. These measures may only concern infant industries, or 'certain sectors undergoing restructuring or facing serious difficulties, particularly where these difficulties produce major social problems'. These measures may not exceed 25 per cent *ad valorem* and must maintain an element of preference for products originating in the Community. Furthermore, the total value of imports of the products which are subject to these measures may not exceed 15 per cent of total imports of industrial products from the Community during the past year for which statistics are available. Also, they cannot be applied for a period exceeding five years unless a longer duration is authorised by the Association Committee.

Such measures cannot be introduced in respect of a product if more than three years have elapsed since the elimination of all duties. When taking such measures Morocco must provide the Association Committee with a schedule for the elimination of customs duties introduced under this Article. This schedule should provide for a phasing out of these duties in equal annual instalments starting at the latest two years after their introduction. The Association Committee may, however, decide on a different schedule. ACP countries will have to formulate their own proposals with regard to the use of safeguard measures within the transitional period, and this arrangement for Morocco should only act as a guide to what would be appropriate.

Arbitration

Where problems arise under the headings of alleged dumping, or matters covered by the safeguard clause, Article 27 requires that the matter be referred to the Association Committee, together with all relevant information, with a view to seeking a solution acceptable to the two parties.

If any other dispute relating to the application or interpretation of the Agreement arises, either party may refer this to the Association Council. The Association Council may settle the dispute by means of a decision. If it is not possible to settle the dispute, then either party may notify the other of the appointment of an arbitrator; the other party must then appoint a second arbitrator within two months. The Association Council then appoints a third arbitrator. The arbitrators' decisions are taken by majority vote. Each party to the dispute must then take the steps required to implement the decision of the arbitrators. In other words, the arbitrators' decisions are final and binding.

These dispute settlement procedures appear to go beyond WTO disciplines in that, although these have been greatly strengthened by the Uruguay Round decision to change from a 'consensus to accept' a disputes panel report to a 'consensus to reject', a party to a dispute may refuse to implement the panel's decision if they are willing to accept retaliation (although such a refusal would undermine WTO disciplines and is therefore extremely rare). Under the dispute settlement procedures of the Morocco agreement, the Association Council deals with disputes and the majority decision of the arbitrators is binding on both parties, although it is unclear what sanctions may be used if the arbitrators' decisions are not implemented. This is a potentially useful innovation which the ACP may well wish to consider incorporating into any future trade agreement with the EU.

Rules of origin

The rules of origin are essentially similar to those in the Lomé Convention. The basic definition for products using non-originating intermediate products in production is a change of tariff heading, where tariff headings are defined in terms of Harmonised Commodity Description and Coding System (HS) chapters and chapter headings refer to the four-digit HS classification level. There is the usual list of excluded processes (such as simple mixing and simple processing), and qualifying process and value-added criteria for other non-originating products, all of which limit access to the EU market and the potential employment creating effects of the FTA.

The main difference is in the area of cumulation, and this will be important for the ACP if Lomé is replaced by a system of regional and national accords. Bilateral cumulation with the EU is permitted under Article 3 but, surprisingly given the objectives of economic integration in the Mediterranean region, cumulation between the Mediterranean countries is permitted only with Algeria and Tunisia (Article 4). It is possible that wider cumulation will be permitted as the EU progressively signs FTAs with the other Mediterranean countries, but if this is the EU's long-run objective then why are Israel, Cyprus and Turkey not included in the agreement with Morocco? Without such Mediterranean-wide cumulation of origin, the EU's FTAs will generate hub-and-spoke systems of trade agreements, concentrating the benefits from the agreements in the EU.

Also, unlike the Lomé Convention, there is no derogation procedure.

The differences in the rules of origin in the agreement with Morocco compared with those in the Lomé Convention are important, as the EU is committed to the harmonisation of the rules of origin in all of its FTAs. It is essential that the ACP resist any restriction of the already onerous rules of origin which it has to fulfil in order to obtain preferential access to the EU market. For example, confining cumulation of origin to the member States of the regional partnership agreement and excluding other ACP countries, or non-ACP developing countries in the region, would seriously undermine regional integration and the general attractiveness of the region to FDI.

Financial co-operation

The EU negotiating mandate separates the negotiation of REPAs from its proposals for financial co-operation, and only mentions the need for additional aid to assist adjustment to a REPA in the context of special treatment for the least-developed ACP. *All* ACP countries participating in a REPA will, however, need substantial additional adjustment assistance:

❖ to enable them to adjust to unrestricted imports from the EU (both to re-allocate resources to enable potentially competitive firms to increase productivity, and to enable new firms and industries to develop on the basis of lower-priced imports of EU capital and intermediate goods);

❖ to deal with the consequences of the fall in import duties through the provision of short term budgetary assistance and technical assistance to change sources of government revenues;

❖ to assist with the introduction of trade-related policy measures forming part of the agreement (competition policy, harmonisation of standards and mutual recognition of regulatory procedures and other measure which seek to reduce the transactions costs of trade with the EU).

The substantial additional aid required to implement an FTA between a developing and an industrialised country is explicitly recognised in the agreement with Morocco:

❖ in order to ensure a co-ordinated approach to dealing with the exceptional macro-economic and financial problems which could stem from the progressive implementation of agreement, the parties shall closely monitor the development of trade and financial relations between the Community and Morocco as part of the regular economic dialogue established under Title V (Article 77).

The latter part of this statement implies that the aid available under this heading is conditional on Morocco implementing the agreement, and therefore provides the EU with additional leverage over policy making and implementation in

Morocco. Nevertheless, the ACP should seriously consider including in the Framework Agreement an explicit commitment by the EU to provide aid and technical assistance for adjustment to a REPA, *additional* to that provided under existing arrangements for co-operation.

Expected effects of the agreement

As explained above, the costs and benefits of preferential trade agreements are traditionally divided into static, or once-and-for-all, effects and dynamic, or growth-enhancing, effects. The static effects are, in turn, divided into beneficial trade creation effects, which comprise the replacement of inefficient local suppliers by more efficient imports from the partner country (EU), and detrimental trade diversion effects, comprising the replacement of more efficient imports from third countries with less efficient or higher-priced imports from the partner country.

The static effects on Morocco's exports to the EU are widely expected to be minimal, as there are no additional concessions of any significance available for agricultural products and none at all for industrial products.

The beneficial trade creation effects could be significant as the EU accounts for 75 per cent of Morocco's imports of non-oil products. Morocco has, until fairly recently, pursued a policy of indiscriminate protection at high levels and it is generally agreed that this has led to widespread, inefficient, industrial diversification. There are therefore potential welfare and efficiency gains to be obtained by consumers and by producers purchasing investment and intermediate goods. The extent of these gains is however uncertain, as it depends on:

❖ how far EU products can substitute for locally produced goods; and

❖ the pricing behaviour of EU exporters, who may be expected to increase their prices – at least to some degree – to capture some of the duty which they previously paid on goods exported to

Morocco, and in so far as they do so then the welfare and efficiency gains will obviously be more limited.

The trade diversion effects may be modest given the relatively small share of non-EU countries in the non-oil imports of Morocco. Some commentators, however, point out that we would expect all of the EU's exports to Morocco to compete directly with those of other, non-preferred, industrialised countries (for example in machinery, transport equipment, and temperate agricultural products) and, given Morocco's high tariff and non-tariff barriers to trade, this adverse substitution effect could be substantial.

The effect on the balance of trade is unambiguous: exports are not expected to increase in the short term as a result of the agreement, while imports will rise as a result of the trade creation and trade diversion effects. In addition, government revenues will fall both as a result of losing duties previously levied on imports from the EU and because of the diversion of imports from dutiable imports from the rest of the world to non-dutiable imports from the EU. Morocco is therefore expected to require both short-term finance for an increasing balance of payments deficit, and budgetary and technical assistance to fill the shortfall in government revenues and enable the government to diversify its sources of revenue away from a dependence on import taxes.

The static effects on employment are also expected to be negative. Adjustment to increased imports from the EU, to the extent to which they displace local production, will increase unemployment, while falling government revenues may also force cuts in public sector employment. The absence of any significant positive effect on exports means that no compensating increase in employment in the labour intensive agricultural and manufacturing export sector is expected. Paradoxically, the immediate effect of the FTA is therefore expected to increase the pressure of migrant workers seeking employment in the EU, contrary to the objectives of the EU's Mediterranean policy.

Longer-term growth effects are more uncertain, though potentially of greater magnitude. These effects essentially revolve around the enhanced credibility given by the FTA to Morocco's structural adjustment policy and the gains in efficiency in factor and product markets expected to arise from this. The agreement is said to act as an 'anchor' for these policies in that liberalisation is automatically guaranteed by the agreement, while the government of Morocco can blame the EU for the structural adjustment costs involved in opening up the economy to international competition. Improvements in the competitive and institutional environment in Morocco, together with guaranteed access to the EU market, are expected to increase FDI. Indeed, much of the literature on the dynamic gains from trade agreements between industrialised and developing countries emphasises the central role of FDI in generating these dynamic gains, as increased foreign involvement can increase transfers of knowledge and resources on *what* to produce, *how* to produce it, and *where* and *how* to market it. Against this optimistic view, critics argue that EU investment will be much more directed towards the internal EU market (following monetary union) and to the CEECs, which will be much more closely integrated into Europe. Much of the European investment which has taken place in Morocco and Tunisia is export platform investment and natural-resource-based investment, both having few or no linkages with the local economy. Empirical studies of the clothing industry in Morocco also show that rates of productivity change for domestic firms in sectors with a high incidence of foreign investment were no higher than in sectors dominated by domestic investment, indicating an absence of spill-over effects. Foreign direct and portfolio investment have been of marginal importance in the economy despite prudent macro-economic management and a wide range of legislative and regulatory reforms which have sought to create a friendly environment for private investment. More generally, critics argue that in the context of acquiring technology, the

FTA with the EU runs the risk of diverting imports away from suppliers of best practice technology in non-EU countries.

The conclusion of all studies is that, at best, an FTA should be seen only as a 'stepping stone' to more general trade liberalisation and that if, instead, it is regarded as a substitute for trade liberalisation then the agreement is likely to produce long-term costs rather than benefits.

The South African FTA

The negotiations for an FTA between the EU and South Africa have lasted four years and had still not been completed at the time of writing this report. Hence, the full and final details are not available. However, a certain number of lessons can be learned since they either underline the conclusions drawn from the Morocco example or point to other features that the ACP may need to anticipate in any REPA negotiations.

Unlike the ACP, South Africa started the negotiations from a low position in the EU's hierarchy of preferences. Indeed, at the outset it was accorded only MFN access and, then, only qualified GSP treatment. However, in the final phase of the negotiations it obtained full GSP access.

Because of its poor initial access (and highly competitive exports of items covered by the CAP), South Africa's attempts to obtain good access to the European market were fraught. At one point, the EU's offer for the 'free' trade area was less satisfactory than that already accorded under the GSP. In other words, had South Africa concluded an agreement on that basis, exports of some products would have received better access under the GSP than under the FTA! This confirms the lesson drawn from the Moroccan example, that the EU is unwilling to use these agreements as a vehicle to tackle remaining areas of protectionism. At the same time, however, it points to the unsatisfactory nature of the GSP (which is the EU's threatened alternative to REPAs – see Part 3). Despite the fact that its *current* access under the GSP was superior to the

EU's FTA offer, South Africa continued to negotiate. This may well have been because it recognised that the GSP in its current form is an inherently unsatisfactory basis for market access. Not least, the provisions for graduation on the basis of market share mean that it can be withdrawn as soon as a country becomes significantly competitive in a particular product.

The South African negotiations illustrate the EU's understanding of the various WTO requirements. Whether or not this understanding is upheld subsequently in the WTO remains to be seen. It seems likely that if the EU–South Africa FTA is concluded, it will pass through WTO scrutiny before any REPAs. Hence, any decision taken on the basis of the EU–South Africa FTA is likely to establish 'case law' which would then apply to REPAs.

Two of the salient requirements of the WTO are that an FTA should cover 'substantially all' trade, and that it should be completed within a 'reasonable period of time'. The EU has clearly interpreted 'substantially all' as meaning 90 per cent of the items currently traded between the two partners. In other words:

❖ the exclusion of products that are not currently traded does not count against the agreement meeting the necessary 90 per cent target;

❖ the 90 per cent figure applies to aggregate trade, and so can comprise more than 90 per cent of one partner's exports offsetting less than 90 per cent of the other partner's.

This suggests that it may well be possible for the ACP to include significant exemptions in any liberalisation offer they make under a REPA. As noted above, this would still be subject to WTO scrutiny, but at least during the negotiations for a REPA it ought to be possible, on the basis of the South Africa precedent, for ACP countries to exclude their most sensitive products from liberalisation. In the South African example, such products have been put into protocols which require further negotiation before any liberalisation is agreed.

The EU has also given a clear indication during the negotiations that it is prepared to consider both asymmetrical liberalisation (with South Africa liberalising later in the implementation period) and for implementation to occur over a period extending up to 12 years. The WTO rubric is that 'a reasonable period of time' should 'normally' be not more than ten years; if this is the norm, then it appears logical to assume that there could be abnormal periods greater than this. Once again, this should ease the adjustment problems of ACP members of REPAs.

There are, however, some less satisfactory features of the EU–South Africa FTA. One is that, as in its mandate for the successor to Lomé negotiations, the EU has introduced areas of non-merchandise trade into its demands. There are sections in the EU–South Africa FTA on services trade and on the free movement of capital. In neither case does it *appear at the present time* that there have been firm and onerous commitments, but it is clear that:

❖ the EU wishes to extend its agreements in these areas;

❖ it may be necessary for any ACP REPA negotiators to exercise extreme caution in ensuring that firm commitments are not introduced into the agreements.

In addition, the EU has used the leverage provided by the negotiations to attempt to force the pace on other trade matters outside the FTA. This includes the negotiation of a fisheries agreement between the EU and South Africa, and also South African recognition of trademarks and origin denominations. The latter is specifically mentioned in the Commission's negotiating mandate for the successor to the Lomé Convention. In the case of fisheries, South Africa appears to have refused to link negotiations, but it appears also to be willing to concede ground on origin denomination (over the designation of sherry and port).

Finally, the provisions in the EU–South Africa FTA on origin rules may set an unwelcome precedent for the ACP. The EU–South Africa FTA uses a system for establishing originating status that is significantly different from that employed both under the Lomé Convention and under the GSP (and the EU's other trade accords). It needs to be established, as a matter of priority, whether the EU–South Africa FTA is a precedent for the system that Europe will attempt to apply to any post-Lomé REPA.

The EU-proposed origin rules for its FTA with South Africa contain a detailed list of products and specify the value-added or processes that are required in respect of each to transform non-originating materials into originating products. Because the origin rules vary from product to product, it is not possible to state whether the EU–South Africa FTA rules are more or less onerous overall than are those under Lomé. However, a comparison is possible on a product-by-product basis. In order to keep the illustrative comparison within reasonable limits, a detailed analysis has been made of the overlap between the items exported to the EU by South Africa on the one hand and by its partners in the Southern African Customs Union (SACU) (Botswana, Lesotho, Namibia and Swaziland) on the other. The results of this analysis are shown in Table 9. This takes the principal items where both South Africa and one of its SACU partners export to the EU and where the EU–South Africa FTA proposes to improve South Africa's access. It then compares the origin rules for these items under the Lomé Convention and under the EU–South Africa FTA. It would appear that in most cases the rules are the same, although for a small number those under the EU–South Africa FTA may be more onerous.

Table 9. Differences between the Lomé and proposed EU–SA FTA origin rules

| CN 1996 | Description (abbreviated) | Working or processing required to be carried out on non-originating products in order that the product manufactured can obtain originating status | | More/less onerous for S. Africa |
		EU proposal	Lomé	
03026965 03037810 03037981 03037996 03042057 03042096 03049047	fresh or chilled hake frozen hake 'merluccius spp.' frozen monkfish saltwater fish, edible, frozen n.e.s. frozen fillets of hake 'merluccius' frozen fillets of saltwater fish, n.e.s. frozen meat of hake 'merluccius', whether or not minced (excl. fillets)	Manufacture in which all the materials of Ch. 3 used must be wholly obtained	Manufacture in which all the materials of Ch. 3 used must already be originating	Same
08052029 08054090 08061029 08061069	fresh or dried tangelos, ortaniques, etc., from 1 March to 31 October fresh or dried grapefruit, from 1 May to 31 October fresh table grapes, from 1 January to 14 July fresh table grapes, from 21 November to 31 December	Manufacture in which: • All the fruit and nuts used must be wholly obtained • The value of any materials of Ch. 17 used does not exceed 30% of the value of the ex-works price of the product		Same
16041319	sardines, prepared or preserved, whole or in pieces	Manufacture from animals of Ch. 1. All the materials of Ch. 3 used must be wholly obtained	Manufacture in which all the fish or fish eggs used must already be originating	Same
17031000	cane molasses resulting from the extraction or refining of sugar	[if flavoured or coloured] Manufacture in which the value of any materials of Ch. 17 used does not exceed 30% of the ex-works price of the product [otherwise] Manufacture in which all the materials used are classified within a heading other than that of the product	[if flavoured or coloured] Manufacture in which the value of any materials of Ch. 17 used does not exceed 30% of the ex-works price of the product	Same?
20082059 20082079 20082099 20094099	pineapples, prepared or preserved, sugar content of =< 17%, packings of > 1 kg pineapples, prepared or preserved, sugar content of =< 19%, packings of =< 1 kg pineapples, prepared or preserved, in packings of < 4.5 kg pineapple juice, density of =< 1.33 g/ccm at 20.C	Manufacture in which: • All the materials used are classified within a heading other than that of the product. • The value of any materials of Ch. 17 used does not exceed 30% of the ex-works price of the product.	Manufacture in which all the materials used are classified in a heading other than that of the product, provided the value of any materials of Ch. 17 used does not exceed 30% of the ex-works price of the product	More?
54025290	filament yarn of polyester	Manufacture from chemical materials or textile pulp	Manufacture from chemical materials or textile pulp	Same

CN 1996	Description (abbreviated)	Working or processing required to be carried out on non-originating products in order that the product manufactured can obtain originating status		More/less onerous for S. Africa
		EU proposal	Lomé	
61091000	t-shirts, singlets and other vests of cotton, knitted or crocheted	Manufacture from yarn [a, b]	Manufacture from yarn [c]	?
62034231	men's or boys' trousers of cotton denim (excl. knitted or crocheted)			
62034235	men's or boys' trousers cotton (excl. knitted or crocheted)			
62034290	men's or boys' shorts of cotton (excl. knitted or crocheted)			
84714190	data-processing machines, automatic, digital, comprising at least a CPU, plus one input/one output unit	Manufacture in which the value of all the materials used does not exceed 40% of the ex-works price of the product	Manufacture in which the value of all the materials used does not exceed 40% of the ex-works price of the product	Same

Notes:

The notes in respect of these products are very long. Notes (a)–(c) provide a summary of some key points.

(a) The conditions set out here shall not be applied to any basic textile materials used in the manufacture of this product which, taken together, represent 10% or less of the total weight of all the basic textile materials used. However, this applies only to mixed products made from two or more of the basic textile materials listed in Note 5.2 to Annex I of the Protocol Concerning the Definition of the Concept of 'Originating Products' and Methods of Administrative Cooperation.

(b) Textile materials, with the exception of linings and interlinings, which do not satisfy the rules set out here for the made-up product concerned may be used provided that they are classified in a heading other than that of the product and that their value does not exceed 8% of the ex-works price of the product.

(c) Textile trimmings and accessories which do not satisfy the rule set out here for the made up products concerned may be used provided that their weight does not exceed 10% of the total weight of all the textile materials incorporated. Textile trimmings and accessories are those classified in Chs 50?63. Linings and interlinings are not regarded as trimmings or accessories.

Sources: Protocol concerning the Definition of the Concept of 'Originating Products' and Methods of Administrative Co-operation, European Commission (no date); Agreement Amending the Fourth ACP–EC Convention of Lomé, signed in Mauritius on 4 November 1995, Protocol 1, Annex II.

Part 3

A Proposal for a Strategy in the WTO Context

The ACP group has indicated that some members may consider the proposal to agree REPAs on its merits when further details are known, but that regardless of this a WTO waiver for the current trade regime should be obtained for a longer period than the five years proposed by the EU. This part of the report analyses the issues involved in obtaining a long waiver. Since this may not be a straightforward exercise, the report then describes a possible parallel strategy for the ACP. This would involve seeking improvements to the GSP so that it could become either an acceptable alternative to Lomé or, at least, a 'safety net' in case the negotiations on a REPA or alternative ACP proposal prove to be unsatisfactory. Finally, the report ends with an analysis of the factors that should be taken into account in drafting the Framework Agreement.

The WTO Waiver

If the ACP are to obtain a waiver for the period 2000–2010, they must convince both the EU (who are willing to apply for a waiver only to 2005) and the WTO member States that such a waiver is justified, and build a constituency within the EU and WTO to support such a proposal. This will not be easy. The EU's objections to a ten-year extension of Lomé arise from the following considerations.

First, a number of member States object, in principle, to the discriminatory nature of Lomé and the extension of Lomé preferences to the least-developed States has not removed this objection.

Second, Lomé preferences are generally perceived to have failed to stimulate and diversify ACP exports to any significant extent. An important perceived reason for this has been the failure of many of the ACP States to liberalise their import regimes, and so reduce the very high levels of discrimination against the export sector. REPAs are envisaged as a way of overcoming the trade policy inertia of these ACP States, and of pushing them towards more outward-oriented trade policies.

Third, the strengthening of the WTO rules-based system of international trade, notably by changing the disputes procedures from 'consensus to accept' to 'consensus to reject' Disputes Panel findings, has meant that the cost to the EU of continuing Lomé has greatly increased in terms of concessions to non-Lomé countries. The EU is unwilling to pay this price, because of the significant internal adjustment costs arising from the introduction of the single European currency and enlargement towards Eastern Europe, both coming at a time of reduced political support for the ACP.

Fourth, the EU has become increasingly concerned about the proliferation of regional preferential trade agreements and the possibility of significant trade diversion against EU exports. They are therefore much more concerned than in the past that such arrangements should be fully compatible with WTO rules (and the CAP) and seeking a ten-year waiver for Lomé is seen as weakening this stance.

The WTO is also a different organisation from the previous GATT, not only in emphasising a rule-based system for international trade, but also in its membership, with most developing countries and countries in Eastern Europe being either members or in the process of applying for membership of the WTO. The most important reason for membership is to be able to defend their trade interests and influence future decisions on trade and trade-related issues. A waiver for Lomé will therefore be more critically examined than in the past.

There are currently (as updated by the WTO on 27 November 1998) 55 ACP members of the WTO (and a further seven countries who have applied for membership); with the 15 EU member States, the ACP–EU group comprises 53 per cent of the present 132 WTO Member States. Technically, a waiver would currently require agreement by a further 29 WTO Member States to achieve a three-quarters majority, but in practice the WTO seeks to achieve consensus and this would also provide greater security for a waiver. In addition, a further 29 non-ACP countries have applied for membership of the WTO and most, if not all, can be expected to become members over the period 2000–2010.

The ACP must consider ways in which a waiver would be most acceptable to the member States of the WTO. Five actions could assist this process.

One would be to support the Ruggiero initiative. The ACP could join with the least-developed in persuading the EU to make its Lomé-equivalent GSP offer to these countries part of its binding commitments on the WTO, so as to provide greater certainty and predictability to these preferences.

Second, the ACP could take the lead in producing firm proposals to 'simplify and review the rules of origin, including cumulation provisions' for the least-developed (EU Council, 1998, n. 8, p. 18). This would help to remove one of the main weaknesses of the GSP as compared with Lomé.

Third, the ACP could take the lead in pressing the EU to make the GSP for these countries *fully* Lomé-equivalent in respect of other differences. This would include the terms of product coverage (in particular, including products subject to tariff quotas), tolerance thresholds, cumulation and derogation provisions.

Fourth, it is probably essential that the ACP clearly demonstrate that a second waiver is not simply a means of extending Lomé preferences into the next century, but is necessary to provide a sufficient period of time for them to adjust to a more competitive environment. A key element in such an adjustment process is for the ACP to *bind their tariff at applied rates* (not simply at the notionally high rates which are currently registered by many ACP countries with the WTO) and to give commitments to progressively lowering barriers to trade. Such a commitment would not only signal a clear intention to liberalise trade with all the member States of the WTO, but is also essential if the ACP are to achieve the objective of a 'gradual and smooth integration of each country into the international economy' (ACP *Negotiating Mandate*, para. 9).

Finally, the ACP need to obtain the best possible legal and technical advice to ensure that a waiver provides legal exemption from *all* of the WTO obligations with which Lomé preferences may be in conflict. The problems of the present waiver were clearly demonstrated by the Disputes Panel on bananas, which noted that the waiver lacked precision. This is a fundamental weakness. The panel emphasised that the waiver (and any future waiver) should be narrowly interpreted to allow only measures *specifically* required by the Convention and precisely covered by the terms of the waiver.

The specific point at issue was that the preamble to the Lomé waiver required that the preferential treatment should not raise undue difficulties for the trade of other countries. The panel ruled that the import licensing procedures for bananas did create 'undue difficulty' and that the Convention did not *specifically* require the licensing procedures (as other means were available to the EU to meet its obligations under Lomé). The panel found that the EU was in violation of its obligations under Article I:1, III:4, X:3 of GATT, Article 1.2 of the Licensing Agreement and Articles II and XVII of the GATS.

To provide a solid and complete legal defence for discriminatory, preferential treatment, the waiver needs to specify *exactly* which:

❖ sections of the Convention need to be covered (including those providing for country specific tariff quotas and for new lines of preferences, such as Articles 168.2b and c);

❖ WTO obligations need to be waived.

A carefully constructed waiver, accepted by consensus, would then provide the ACP countries with legally secure preferences. But this may be difficult to achieve. It would be prudent, therefore, for the ACP to consider pursuing alternative options in parallel. The next section considers the scope for improving the GSP.

The Feasibility of an Enhanced GSP

The GSP as an option for the ACP States

The EU has proposed the GSP as an alternative option for those non-LDC States unable to enter into FTAs. The ACP, in its negotiating mandate, has correctly stated that this option is not attractive to the ACP. In addition to being less generous than the current Lomé provisions, the ACP also note that the GSP is a unilateral and discretionary offer provided by the EU but not subject to any negotiation or representation by the beneficiary countries and that it involves certain restrictions.

The EU, however, is committed to examining:

❖ all alternative possibilities in order to provide these countries with a new framework for trade between them and the European Union which is equivalent to their existing situation under the Lomé Convention and in conformity with WTO rules. In particular the Council and the Commission will take into account their interest in the review of the GSP in 2004, making use of the differentiation permitted by WTO rules (EU Council, 1998, p. 18, n. 8).

This, of course, does not commit the EU to providing standard GSP access equivalent to Lomé, not least because to be WTO-compatible it would have to be offered to all equivalent developing countries, which may well be unacceptable to at least some EU member States. This is because it would involve providing duty-free access on very sensitive and sensitive products which are currently either excluded from the EU's GSP offer, or are subject only to very small tariff reductions.

There is a difference, however, between accepting the EU's current standard GSP as an acceptable post-Lomé option (which it clearly is not) and seeking to identify improvements that could make the scheme a reasonable 'safety net' (in case other options fail) which are potentially feasible politically. It is argued that it is in the interests of the ACP to examine the possibilities of a differentiated GSP offering a credible alternative to an FTA. Despite its shortcomings, the GSP – if sufficiently improved – could have some advantages over a REPA. As explained in Part 2, REPAs imply – at least for a number of the ACP countries, particularly in sub-Saharan Africa – substantial costs with only limited possibilities for these to be offset by long-term, dynamic, growth-enhancing advantages. For these countries the trade diversion costs are likely to be greater than the trade creation benefits. An FTA would also tie them even more closely to Europe than is currently the case, when their need is to diversify their export markets. Regional FTAs would also add to existing barriers to increasing intra-regional trade and create a 'hub and spoke' system (see above), concentrating the gains from trade into the hands of EU exporters and investors.

In contrast, use of an improved GSP for preferential access to the EU would leave the ACP free to pursue their own independent trade strategies both with respect to the EU and other potential trade partners outside the region and with respect to deepening trade relations within the region. Whilst the GSP would be unlikely to improve on Lomé, the analysis of the EU's FTA with Morocco, discussed in Part 2, showed that the EU was unwilling to provide additional benefits beyond those previously obtaining in the bilateral non-reciprocal agreements. And the analysis of the EU–South Africa FTA reinforces the view that the EU will be reluctant to agree substantially improved access under a REPA. In particular, the EU was not willing in the Morocco agreement to provide additional preferences in agricultural products, despite their importance in generating employment as well as export earnings and the EU's undoubted wish to improve the economic growth and stability of the Mediterranean region.

If the ACP are to negotiate better terms than the Mediterranean countries and South Africa, they will need a credible alternative to a REPA to strengthen their negotiating position. An extension of the Lomé Convention for a further period of 10 to 15 years as envisaged in the ACP negotiating mandate, sanctioned by additional WTO waivers, would provide one alternative. But the EU have indicated their extreme reluctance, at the very least, to agree to such a long-term extension of Lomé. Furthermore, even if the EU were willing to try to obtain the necessary waivers in the WTO the price of doing so might be unacceptable to the EU, or it might simply be impossible to obtain. Indeed, an over-reliance by the ACP on including within the Framework Agreement a commitment to seek a ten-year waiver is risky. Without a guarantee on market access even in the event of a waiver not being granted, it would make the ACP vulnerable to a decision in the WTO which they are not overly well placed to influence.

An enhanced and suitably differentiated GSP could thus provide the only credible alternative for maintaining ACP preferential access to the EU. But is it feasible? One of the difficulties in the way of the ACP obtaining an improved GSP is that the responsibility within the Commission does not rest with DG VIII and cannot therefore be directly negotiated with them. Since, however, the EU is committed to examining all alternative possibilities for using differentiation in the GSP to provide the non-least-developed ACP countries with Lomé-equivalent access, then this ought not to be an obstacle to the ACP stating their requirements. A less tractable potential problem is to identify a set of criteria for an enhanced GSP that would be acceptable to the EU and, very importantly, to the WTO members, whilst providing Lomé-style benefits to the ACP (and not to their competitors). It is to this problem that the section is devoted.

Improvements to the GSP rules of origin

One area in which the GSP would have to be improved to give equivalent access to access under Lomé is in respect of the rules of origin. It is in the interest of the ACP as well as the EU to ensure that non-beneficiaries of the scheme are excluded from preferences. The purpose of rules of origin is to ensure that this differentiation between beneficiaries and non-beneficiaries is maintained in EU imports. It has, however, long been a source of complaint that the EU goes beyond this legitimate purpose of rules of origin and uses them as a non-tariff barrier to preferential imports from the developing countries.

Goods which are derived from inputs wholly produced within a beneficiary State are clearly originating products, and the problem of definition arises only when exports to the EU from a beneficiary are produced from inputs which, to some degree, originate from other countries. The EU has approached this problem in a number of ways. In common with all countries granting tariff preferences the problem of defining an originating product starts with the concept that a final product must have undergone 'sufficient working or processing' in the country receiving preferences. All goods entering into international trade have been classified, for customs purposes, under the Harmonised Commodity Description and Coding System (HS). The HS has 96 chapters for traded goods, divided into 1,242 4-digit headings. This tariff classification has the advantages of (a) providing an agreed international definition of products and (b) reflecting a substantial change to the characteristics of a product as between one tariff heading and another.

The tariff schedule was not, however, drawn up specifically to provide a definition of sufficient working or processing. The EU has therefore supplemented the tariff jump criterion to cover cases where there has been a change in the 4-digit tariff heading but insufficient transformation. These conditions can be classified into four categories:

❖ excluded processes – where the transformation of the non-originating materials does not confer originating status, for example simple assembly;

❖ **process criteria** – which specifies stages of production that must be undertaken to provide originating status;

❖ **percentage criteria** – where the value of the non-originating materials used must not exceed a given per centage of the ex works price of the finished product (usually either 40 per cent or 50 per cent). This is sometimes supplemented by the further condition that the value of the non-originating materials used should not exceed the value of the originating materials used, or that particular non-originating materials should not exceed 10 per cent of the ex works price of the product.

❖ **a combination** of process and value-added criteria.

Given the very detailed differences between the GSP rules and those in Lomé it is not practical to make a comparison across the board, but the most important imports from beneficiaries have been used to identify illustrative differences. For example, one of the most important product groups is knitwear (Chapter 61). The Lomé rules of origin permit such articles to be classified as originating in an ACP State even if they are produced from non-originating imported yarn (which is classified under a variety of 4-digit headings which are outside Chapter 61). In other words it requires a single tariff jump. But the GSP rules require a double tariff jump since the only non-originating imported input that is allowed is fibre (which must then be spun in the GSP State).

There are also differences, but less marked ones, in relation to woven clothing (Chapter 62). Whereas the GSP rules always require a double tariff jump (since yarn, which must then be woven, is the only acceptable non-originating input), the Lomé rules provide an alternative. Under Lomé the non-originating input can be either yarn or uncoated fabric (i.e. a single tariff jump) provided this does not exceed 40 per cent of the price of the product.

Such differences are not limited to clothing. In the case of video recorders, for example, the percentage criteria in Lomé are lower than those under the GSP. The standard rule for the products of most importance under the GSP (heading 8521) combines percentage criteria (the value of all the materials used must not exceed 40 per cent of the price, and the non-originating ones must not exceed the value of the originating ones) and also a process criterion (all transistors used must be originating). Under Lomé, by contrast, there is the same 40 per cent criterion but no process criterion. Instead the Lomé rules stipulate only that the non-originating inputs within the same heading must not exceed 10 per cent of the price.

Because the rules apply to products with several components and since many of these components, especially in a developing country, will be imported, they tend to apply more to manufactured than to agricultural goods. However, they may also apply to processed agricultural items, such as fruit juice. The GSP rules do not permit non-originating sugar to be used;

the Lomé rules allow it provided it does not exceed 30 per cent of the price.

The recent problems of Bangladesh (a least-developed country), which would not have occurred if the GSP origin rules on clothing were the same as those under Lomé, illustrate the consequences of over-restrictive provisions. The examples cited demonstrate that this is not an isolated problem.

As in the Lomé Convention, beneficiaries can include imports from the EU as 'originating' products (cumulation) and so potentially making it easier to meet the process and value-added criteria of the rules of origin (compared with importing intermediate products from third countries).

Regional cumulation among beneficiary developing countries is, however, much more restrictive than Lomé and extended only to the Andean countries, CACM (Central American Integration Agreements) and ASEAN (Association of South East Asian Nations) countries, while the rules for regional cumulation are so strict that in practice they are very difficult to comply with. In addition, the new GSP did not include additional regional cumulation despite the Commission's request to include South Asia, Mercosur and ALADI (Latin America). Also, the scope for including EU content in production is limited by the fact that GSP origin rules are used to determine Community origin.

Derogations from the rules of origin are available to the least-developed countries (since 1984), but these are less generous than Lomé which provides for longer periods for derogations, a greater number of grounds on which derogations can be requested, and time limits for an EU response. The EU is, however, committed to reviewing the rules of origin for the least-developed countries with a view to simplification and including cumulation provisions.

The rules of origin include a tolerance threshold for ignoring non-originating material but – unlike Lomé, where this threshold has been set at 15 per cent – the GSP sets the level at 5 per cent, and this does not apply to textiles.

The 'cost' of the ACP transferring to the GSP

Table 2 provided details of the loss of preferences, analysed by the most important ACP exports to the EU, the major ACP exporters, and the loss of foreign exchange consequential on replacing Lomé with the GSP. This section extends the analysis to consider the likely position of the most important ACP exports if Lomé preferences were not renewed after 2005.

The special problems of protocol products
Sugar

One of the most valuable preferences, available to 13 ACP countries, has been the Sugar Protocol which, as shown in Table 2, has provided a foreign exchange equivalent of Ecu 470 million or 61 per cent of the total foreign exchange equivalent available to the ACP. The value of these preferences, however, seems certain to fall substantially and indeed the EU has suggested that they may disappear completely if the ACP countries concerned were to rely solely on the GSP.

First, the EU's duty on unrefined sugar imports will fall to Ecu 419 per tonne by 2000, while the additional quota currently available to the ACP for special preferential sugar is likely to be phased out or eliminated after 2000 as the EU adjust to the Uruguay Round Agreement to limit subsidised exports of sugar. These two factors together will reduce the value of tariff revenue transferred to the ACP countries, and if the EU were to reduce the internal EU support price in line with cuts in import duties (a further round of which could be agreed by 2004/5 during the next round of multilateral negotiations on agriculture which are scheduled to begin in 1999) then ACP sugar export revenues will be substantially reduced.

Second, the future for these preferential tariff quotas is uncertain. Under Article 1 of the Protocol, the EU is committed:

❖ for an indefinite period, to purchase and import at guaranteed prices 1,294,700 tonnes of cane sugar a year from the ACP States and in the event of the Convention ceasing to be operative, the sugar supplying States . . . and the Community shall adopt the appropriate institutional provisions to ensure the continued application of the provisions of this Protocol.

The provisions of the Protocol may be denounced by the Community at two years' notice (Article 10) but an Annex to the Convention states that this provision is 'for the purpose of juridical security and does not represent for the Community any qualification or limitation of the principles enunciated in Article 1 of [the] Protocol'.

This security of access would appear to have been reinforced by the current access tariff quota commitments by the EU in the Uruguay Round Agreements, including the Agreement on Agriculture which lists 'ACP 1,297,700 tonnes in accordance with the provisions of the Lomé Convention'. Despite this apparent double-barrelled security of market access, the future of the Sugar Protocol has been questioned by some Commission officials who have argued that the EU can denounce the Sugar Protocol and that the reference to the Lomé Convention in the Agreement on Agriculture means that if Lomé (and its WTO waiver) ceases in 2005 then so too does the EU's obligations under the current access tariff quota commitments for ACP sugar. The alternative view is that the reference to provisions of the Lomé Convention simply refers to the arrangements for the distribution of the tariff quota between the beneficiary ACP States and not to the overall quota, which will exist independently of Lomé and its waiver.

A further potential threat to the Sugar Protocol has arisen from the WTO Disputes Panel decision on bananas (see Part 1 of this report), which implicitly challenges the legality of country-specific tariff quotas. The panel stated, *inter alia*, on this issue that 'we conclude that the EC's inclusion of allocations [of country-specific tariff quotas] is inconsistent with the requirements of Article XIII in its schedule and does not prevent them from being challenged by other members'. Since Article XIII reflects the MFN clause, and specifies that tariff quotas should, as closely as possible, represent 'the shares which the various contracting parties might be expected to obtain in the absence of such restrictions' (XIII.2), it follows that the country-specific tariff quotas of the Sugar Protocol are potentially subject to challenge as violating Article I and Article XIII of GATT.

An additional potential challenge in the WTO is to the EU's exclusion from its Uruguay Round declaration on subsidised sugar exports of an amount equivalent to imports of ACP sugar. If successful, it is likely that the EU would seek to offset the costs of adjustment of further decreases in exports of subsidised sugar by decreasing imports from the ACP countries.

All of these uncertainties regarding the future for preferential exports of sugar to the EU market pose difficult policy dilemmas for those ACP States for which exports of sugar to the EU constitute a significant proportion of total export earnings. In the long term world trade in sugar will approximate to a free market, and in the meantime these States would be advised to tax the economic rents accruing to exporters and use this revenue to assist the diversification of exports. In the meantime, if the Sugar Protocol is unable to continue after 2005 then preferential access can only be obtained either through differential treatment within the GSP, or by concluding an FTA with the EU which would include exports of sugar.

Bananas

As explained in Part 1 of this report, the EU's attempt to cross-subsidise traditional ACP fruit by allocating import licences for dollar-area bananas to ACP shippers and allowing them to sell these import licences to shippers of dollar-zone fruit has been stopped by the WTO Disputes Panel finding. The effect of this has been to call into question the viability of ACP exports of bananas, even with tariff preferences. Furthermore, the new tariff quota arrangements have been declared unacceptable by the USA which, in November 1998, threatened retaliation against EU exports to the USA. Clearly the controversy over bananas has not ceased, and it is unfortunate that the ACP suppliers have been caught up in a much wider controversy regarding the new rule-based system of the WTO.

If the Lomé Convention ceased to exist, either in 2000 because of a failure to renew the WTO waiver, or in 2005, then this would further weaken the EU's case for giving tariff preferences to ACP suppliers. The Disputes Panel clearly stated that 'the EC has only one regime for banana imports for the purposes of analysing whether its allocation of tariff quota shares is consistent with the requirements of Article XIII' (Non-discriminatory Administration of Quantitative Restrictions). If Lomé ceases to exist, then it would appear inevitable that the separate tariff quota for traditional ACP suppliers would also be unacceptable in the WTO. Paragraph 2(d) of Article XIII may provide some protection for ACP suppliers, in that it states that:

❖ in cases in which a quota is allocated among supplying countries the contracting parties applying the restrictions may seek agreement with respect to the allocation of shares in the quota with all other contracting parties having a substantial interest in supplying the product concerned. In cases in which this method is not reasonably practicable, the contracting party concerned shall allot to contracting parties having a substantial interest in supplying the product shares based upon the proportions, supplied by such contracting parties during the previous representative period, of the total quantity or value of imports of the product, due account being taken of any special factors which may have affected or may be affecting the trade in the product.

Clearly the interpretation and application of this provision would be open to considerable debate, not least regarding the ability or otherwise of the EU to allot tariff quotas, and what would be acceptable as a 'representative period' on which such tariff quotas would be based. As in the case of sugar, if preferential tariff quotas are unable to continue after 2000, then the only WTO-compatible routes available to banana exporters are either differential treatment within the GSP (an unlikely proposition) or the conclusion of an FTA with the EU as, presumably, bananas could be included in the agreement and thus provide legally secure preferential access to the EU market.

Beef

The import regime for beef provides relatively high levels of protection for EU producers and comprises an *ad valorem* duty (currently 15.2 per cent) and a specific duty (currently Ecu 3,603/tonne). Six ACP States share an annual tariff quota of 52,100 tonnes, allocated in particular to Botswana, Namibia, Zimbabwe and Madagascar. As discussed in Part 1, in order to stimulate depressed levels of EU consumption of beef, the EU's internal support prices for beef are scheduled to be reduced by 30 per cent in three annual amounts over the period 2000 to 2002. To compensate for the negative effect which this will have on farmers' income, *Agenda 2000* proposes to increase significantly direct headage payments to farmers. *Agenda 2000* contains no proposals for a reduction in the import tariff on beef, but should this be reduced in line with the cut in the intervention price then this will have two effects on the ACP exports. First, the price which is received will be 30 per cent lower than at present. Second, the decrease in levels of border protection will increase imports from third countries, particularly producers in South America (Argentina, Brazil, Uruguay) which would be highly competitive relative to ACP producers in the EU market.

The problems of least-developed ACP countries

The EU has, as discussed above, promised that the least-developed ACP States that do not enter into a REPA will continue to benefit from access to the EU market equivalent to that which they receive under Lomé. In general terms this might be thought easy to achieve, given that the EU has already offered all least-devel-oped countries Lomé-equivalent access. As we have shown, however, the current GSP offer to the least-developed falls short of Lomé-equivalent access in a number of respects:

❖ it does not cover agricultural products subject to tariff quotas under Lomé;

❖ GSP rules of origin are less favourable;

❖ cumulation provisions are substantially inferior;

❖ tolerance thresholds are substantially lower in the GSP;

❖ derogation procedures are more restrictive than Lomé;

Table 10. Products for which ACP LDDC access could be diminished by GSP treatment

CN 1996	Description (abbreviated)	Exports to EU 1996		Lomé (Q=quota)	Post-UR MFN linked to current GSP		'Forex equiv.'	LDDC exporters
		Ecu 000	Tons		a.v.	specific	Ecu 000	
02023090	frozen bovine boned meat	3,027	1,479	0+446.7 [a]	12.8%	+ 3041 ECU/T	4,885	Madagascar
04069021	cheddar	3,454	1,556	Q 122.7 [a]		1671 ECU/T	2,600	Mozambique
07099060	fresh or chilled sweetcorn	1,119	487	13.6 [a]		94 ECU/T	46	Zambia
07141099	manioc, fresh or dried whole or sliced	426	4,581	11.3 [b]		95 ECU/T	435	Benin
08030019	bananas, fresh (excl. plantains)	10,699	25,121	Q 0; 750 [c]		680 ECU/T	17,082	Somalia
10070090	grain sorghum (excl. hybrid for sowing)	3,498	26,527	Q 3.46 [d]; 4.33 d		94 ECU/T	2,494	Sudan
17011110	raw cane sugar, for refining	19,870	42,304	Q 0; 41 [a]		339 ECU/T	14,341	Malawi, Tanzania Zambia
17011190	raw cane sugar	13,199	19,902	Q 0; 50.7 [a]		419 ECU/T	8,339	Madagascar Malawi
17019910	white sugar	7,757	12,009	Q 0; 50.7 [a]		419 ECU/T	5,032	Madagascar Malawi
17031000	cane molasses	8,697	96,570	Q 0; 0.43 [a]		0.35 ECU/ 100kg	338	Djibouti Mozambique Sudan
22084010	rum and taffia	111	164 [f]	Q 0; 0.9 [e]		0.6 ECU/%vol/hl + 3.2 ECU/hl	1	Haiti

Notes:
(a) Ecum/100 kg/net
(b) Ecua/100kg/net
(c) Ecum/1000kg/net
(d) Ecua/1000 kg
(e) Ecum/%vol/hl + 4.7 Ecum/hl. The quota applies to rum only; taffia is zero.
(f) Hectolitres. The 'forex equivalent' has been calculated on the Ecu/hl element of the specific duty only, and on the assumption that the exports were of rum.
Sources: Eurostat 1997; Taric 1996; WTO 1996.

- ❖ the safeguard clause is more restrictive;

- ❖ the GSP contains conditionality clauses which are absent from Lomé;

- ❖ preferences for Protocol products, which are substantial, are not included in the GSP.

Table 10 identifies a list of 11 items which are imported from ACP least-developed countries and would face a significant increase in tariff barriers if given current GSP treatment. As can be seen from the column headed 'forex equivalent', the duty that would have to be paid on these imports is substantial. On the assumptions used it would be over Ecu 55.5 million per year for all 11 products. This would particularly affect exports of raw cane sugar for refining (Malawi, Tanzania, Zambia), cane sugar (Madagascar and Malawi), white sugar (Madagascar and Malawi), and grain sorghum (Sudan).

Hence, unless the EU is proposing to have a special tranche of the GSP for ACP least-developed countries, which would appear to face the same problems of international acceptability as the Lomé Convention, it will be necessary to improve the GSP for *all* least-developed countries in order to bring it up to the Lomé level.

This raises the question of whether the improvements would also be extended to the Andean Community countries which currently benefit from very similar preferences to the least developed. If so, these special preferences would appear to be just as vulnerable to international criticism, although it should be noted that the existing arrangements for the Andean and Central American countries are discriminatory and probably violate Article I of the GATT. For example, the rationale for offering these countries special preferences is to assist them in combating the growing of and trafficking in drugs, but the same arguments would surely apply with equal force to a number of Asian countries.

It is clear, therefore, that the current shortfall of the GSP for the least-developed countries is an important policy issue affecting not only the ACP but all least-developed countries. The initial position, however, is likely to be that only ACP countries will be in the position to benefit from an upgrading of the GSP to Lomé equivalence and hence there should be no immediate problems arising from the generalisation of these preferences to other States.

The problems of non-least-developed ACP countries

The provisions of Lomé-equivalent preferences which are also WTO-compatible and contained within the EU's GSP would appear to be the most intractable problem, since there are no internationally agreed conventions which would allow the EU to discriminate exclusively in favour of this group of countries. Is it possible to identify objectively defensible categories that would provide access equivalent to Lomé for the ACP whilst avoiding opening the flood gates to many other developing countries, since this would be unacceptable to the EU?

To enable us to define the dimensions of the problem we can make two assumptions. First, we exclude Protocol products on the basis that continued preferential access for these products probably lies outside of the GSP. Second, we can assume that a tariff increase of 5 per cent or less will have a negligible effect on the volume of exports to the EU. This is because the administrative savings of no longer applying for preferences and complying with the EU's preferential import regime would probably compensate exporters for small increases in import duties; and because the trade creation and trade diversion effects will be insignificant under normal assumptions regarding price elasticities of supply and demand and elasticities of substitution.

On the basis of these assumptions, Table 2 enables us to identify the most affected products and countries. In the case of exports of *fishery and agricultural products*, tuna and skipjack are potentially faced with the highest increase in tariffs and Côte d'Ivoire, Senegal, Mauritius, Ghana,

Seychelles, Fiji and Namibia face the greatest competition from other countries.

Other products faced with a significant increase in tariffs are:

* tobacco, partly or wholly stemmed or stripped, (Zimbabwe);

* frozen hake (Namibia);

* fresh cut roses and buds from 1 November to 31 May (Kenya, Zimbabwe);

* fresh cut flowers and buds from 1 November to 31 May (Kenya, Zimbabwe, Côte d'Ivoire, Mauritius);

* fresh or chilled beans from 1 October to 30 June (Kenya, Senegal, Zimbabwe, Cameroon);

* cocoa paste (Côte d'Ivoire, Cameroon, Ghana).

By far the most important *manufactured goods* affected by a loss of Lomé preferences would be clothing. As explained in Part 1, the most important source of Lomé preferences has been exemption from MFA quotas and these are scheduled to end in 2005. ACP exporters will have to adjust to this substantial loss of preferences by moving up-market into less price-sensitive sectors of the clothing market and by either increasing levels of productivity to match the level of major competitors in Asia or locating the more labour-intensive stages of production into lower labour-cost countries. An example of this process would be Mauritius investment in Madagascar.

An increase from the present duty-free access to the EU market to a tariff of 10.2 per cent would, however, face ACP exporters with additional problems of adjustment, especially in such a price-sensitive market. This would particularly affect Mauritius and Jamaica, but also a long list of ACP countries which at present export small quantities of clothing to the EU, but some of which may well be able to expand their exports if preferences were allowed to continue.

Making the GSP more differentiated

As currently structured, the GSP produces anomalous results. There is no clear developmental or economic basis for the differential access given to various sub-groups. But changing from the *status quo* to something that is more justifiable is no easy task.

This section provides an illustration of the potential implications of adopting three different criteria for differential treatment within the GSP, with the objective of enabling the non-least-developed ACP countries to retain their existing market access to the EU.

Income-based differentiation

This section provides an empirical illustration of the potential implications of adopting an income-based differentiation in which the EU recognises five categories of country (apart from those which have negotiated FTA-type arrangements): MFN, three classes of standard GSP (upper, normal, lower), and the least-developed countries. Such a differentiation would potentially allow the EU to continue to offer at least to the poor non-least-developed ACP countries (as well as to the least-developed countries) Lomé-type access without extending this to medium-income States.

This three-way standard GSP classification has been applied to the results of the analysis of ACP trade data in Part 1. Figures on important EU imports from the non-least-developed ACP and their most important competitors have been sorted to show the income group into which the supplying countries would fall. The income cut-offs adopted for this exercise are:

* MFN – States with a GNP per head (1995) of $5,000 or above;

* upper-income GSP – States with a GNP per head of $3,300-$4,999;

* normal GSP – States with a GNP per head of $500-$3,299

* low-income GSP – States with a GNP the head of below $500.

The evidence from this exercise shows that such a reform would benefit only three non-least-developed ACP countries (Ghana, Nigeria and Kenya) unless Lomé access were accorded to the 'normal' as well as 'poor' countries. But if this were done then many of the ACP's main competitors would also benefit (Table 11).

Table 11. Implications for non-LDDC ACP of systematic income differentiation within the GSP

CN 1995	Short description	Exporters [a]			
		MFN	Upper-income	Normal-income	Low-income
02013000	fresh/chilled beef, boneless	Argentina, Uruguay	Brazil	Zimbabwe, Namibia, Botswana	
03026996	saltwater fish, edible, fresh/chilled		Trinidad/Tobago, Mauritius	Senegal, C.d'Ivoire, Jamaica, Namibia, PNG, Zimbabwe Morocco, Croatia, Turkey	Ghana, Nigeria, Kenya
03037810	frozen hake 'merluccius spp.'	Argentina	Chile	Namibia S. Africa	
03042057	frozen fillets of hake 'merluccius'	Argentina	Chile	Namibia, Senegal Peru	
03061390	frozen shrimps and prawns		Gabon, Trinidad/Tobago	Senegal, C.d'Ivoire, Congo Rep., Cameroon Thailand, Ecuador	Nigeria, Kenya, Ghana India
06031051	roses, 1 Nov.–31 May	Israel	Mauritius	Zimbabwe, Senegal, C.d'Ivoire Ecuador, Colombia	Kenya, Nigeria
06031069	flowers, 1 Nov.–31 May	Israel	Mauritius	Zimbabwe, C.d'Ivoire, Jamaica, Namibia, Cameroon, Dom. Rep. Ecuador, S. Africa	Kenya, Nigeria
07082010	beans 'vigna spp./phaseolus spp.', 1 Oct.–30 June			Senegal, Zimbabwe, Cameroon, Dom. Rep., C.d'Ivoire Egypt, Morocco, Turkey	Kenya, Nigeria, Ghana
08030019	bananas, fresh		Gabon	Cameroon, C.d'Ivoire, Jamaica, Dom. Rep. Ecuador, Costa Rica, Colombia	Ghana, Kenya
08043000	fresh/dried pineapples		Mauritius Brazil	C.d'Ivoire, Dom. Rep., Cameroon, Zimbabwe, Senegal S. Africa, Thailand	Ghana, Kenya, Nigeria
15081090	crude groundnut oil	Argentina, USA	Brazil Gabon	Senegal PNG, C.d'Ivoire,	Nigeria Ghana, Nigeria
15111090	crude palm oil		Malaysia, Brazil	Cameroon, Senegal Indonesia	
16041414	tunas/skipjack prepared/preserved in vegetable oil		Mauritius	C.d'Ivoire, Senegal, Namibia Thailand, Philippines, Turkey	Ghana
16041418	tunas/skipjacks, prepared or preserved		Mauritius	C.d'Ivoire, Senegal, Namibia Thailand, Philip-pines, Colombia	Ghana

CN 1995	Short description	Exporters [a]			
		MFN	Upper-income	Normal-income	Low-income
17011110	raw cane sugar, for refining		Mauritius, Trinidad/ Tobago *Brazil*	Jamaica, Zimbabwe, Congo Rep.	
17011190	raw cane sugar (not for refining)		Mauritius *Brazil*	Zimbabwe *S. Africa*	Nigeria
18031000	cocoa paste	*Norway*	*Brazil*	C.d'Ivoire, Cameroon, Dom. Rep. *Indonesia*	Ghana, Nigeria
18040000	cocoa butter, fat and oil		*Malaysia, Brazil*	C.d'Ivoire, Cameroon, Dom. Rep. *Indonesia*	Ghana, Nigeria
21011011	extracts of coffee	*Switzerland*	*Brazil*	C.d'Ivoire, Senegal *Colombia*	Ghana, Nigeria
22084090	rum and taffia		*Trinidad/Tobago Brazil*	Jamaica, C.d'Ivoire	
24012010	flue-cured Virginia-type tobacco	*USA, Argentina*	Trinidad/Tobago *Brazil*	Zimbabwe	Ghana, Kenya, Nigeria
28182000	aluminium oxide	*USA, Australia*	*Hungary*	Jamaica	
29051100	methanol		Trinidad/Tobago	*Russia, Venezuela*	
41051210	sheep/lambskin leather	*Saudi Arabia*	*Brazil*	Cameroon *Algeria*	Nigeria, Kenya
41061200	goat/kidskin leather			Cameroon, C.d'Ivoire, Dom. Rep. *China*	Nigeria, Kenya *Nepal, Pakistan*
61051000	men's cotton shirts, knitted/crocheted	*Hong Kong*	Mauritius	Dom. Rep., Zimbabwe, Jamaica *Turkey, China*	Nigeria
61091000	T-shirts of cotton		Mauritius, Trinidad/ Tobago	Zimbabwe, C.d'Ivoire, Botswana, Dom. Rep., Jamaica, Senegal` *Turkey*	Kenya, Nigeria *Bangladesh, India*
61101031	men's wool jerseys, etc., knitted/ crocheted	*Hong Kong*	Mauritius	Jamaica, Zimbabwe *Tunisia, Croatia*	
61101091	women's wool jerseys, etc., knitted/ crocheted	*Hong Kong*	Mauritius	Jamaica, Dom. Rep., Namibia *China*	Ghana
61102099	women's cotton jerseys, etc., knitted/ crocheted	*Hong Kong*	Mauritius	Jamaica, Dom. Rep., Zimbabwe, C.d'Ivoire, Senegal *Turkey, China*	Nigeria, Kenya
62052000	men's cotton shirts	*Hong Kong*	Mauritius, Trinidad/ Tobago	Zimbabwe, Jamaica, Dom. Rep., Botswana, C.d'Ivoire, Senegal	Kenya, Nigeria, Ghana *India, Bangladesh*
72024199	ferro-chromium	*Norway*		Zimbabwe *Latvia, Russia*	
76011000	aluminium, unwrought	*Norway, Canada*		Cameroon, C.d'Ivoire, Namibia *Russia*	Ghana

Note: (a) All non-LDDC ACP exporters for which GNP per head data available. Also shown, in italics, are as many of the three largest non-ACP suppliers as GNP data are available for.

Sources: Eurostat 1996; World Bank 1997: Table 1.

For example, in the case of saltwater fish, fresh or chilled, maintaining preferential access for Senegal, Côte d'Ivoire, Jamaica, Namibia, Papua New Guinea and Zimbabwe, would also require the same preferences to be extended to Croatia. Maintaining preferential access for fresh bananas for Cameroon, Côte d'Ivoire, Jamaica and the Dominican Republic would also require the same preferences to be offered to Ecuador, Costa Rica, and Colombia. Maintaining preferences for tuna for Côte d'Ivoire, Senegal and Namibia, would require the same preferences to be offered to Thailand and the Philippines. Maintaining preferences for cocoa paste for Côte d'Ivoire, Cameroon and Dominican Republic would require the same preferences to be offered to Indonesia. And maintaining preferences for cut flowers would require the same preferences to be offered to South Africa (a developed country in the WTO).

In addition, this analysis applies only to *existing* ACP exports. It is essential that the ACP countries as a whole participate more fully in international trade and *diversify* their exports into a wider range of products. As they succeed in doing so, it can be expected that the problem identified above, of having to widen preferences to many of the ACP's main competitors, would become more acute. Differentiating the GSP in this way and widening preferential access to the EU market to include a substantial group of Asian and Latin American countries would almost certainly meet with substantial opposition from protectionist lobbies within the EU, and the political acceptability of this proposal must therefore be doubted.

Vulnerability-based differentiation

It has been argued for many years that the conventional measures of growth and economic development are misleading indicators of economic welfare in the presence of vulnerability, as this creates additional risks and uncertainty and thereby inhibits growth and development. These arguments are usually developed in the context of small countries or small-island countries, since these are widely believed to be vulnerable to exposure to external economic forces, environmental catastrophes and remoteness from the mainstream of economic activity.

Recently, the WTO has agreed to consider proposals for the institutionalisation of preferential trade concessions for small-island developing States through an extension of special and differential treatment. The argument for associating volatility with size of the nation state presumes that their greater exposure to external forces compounds the adverse effects of their small size.

In this context, the Commonwealth Secretariat has recently commissioned a report (Atkins *et al.*, 1998) which seeks to construct a vulnerability index which could provide a basis for such special and differential treatment of vulnerable States.

The starting point for constructing the index is that heightened vulnerability is shown in a higher volatility of growth in economic output. Output volatility is measured by the standard deviation of annual rates of growth of constant price *per capita* GDP. This index of output volatility is then used to determine the factors that might lead to vulnerability. These factors are considered to fall within three broad categories: economic exposure; remoteness and insularity; and proneness to environmental events and hazards which impact on the economy.

A model based on three variables was found to be statistically significant: export dependency ratio, merchandise export diversification, and vulnerability to natural disasters. The estimated coefficients for these three variables then form the weights attached to each factor and making up the composite index of vulnerability. To compute this composite index of excess volatility in output growth, observations on an individual country are then imputed into the equation to give a model-based predicted volatility score for that country.

The definition used for small States was countries with a population of 1.5 million or less. In addition, three somewhat larger States – Jamaica, Lesotho and Papua New Guinea – were included in the small State category since it could be argued that they 'share many of the physical and economic characteristics of small States in their respective regions' (Atkins et al., 1998).

The results of this exercise showed that 24 of the 25 most vulnerable States were small States, as defined in the study. The nine most vulnerable States were Vanuatu, Antigua and Barbuda, Tonga, Bahamas, Botswana, Swaziland, Gambia, Maldives and Fiji. Conversely, large States made up all of the 25 least vulnerable States.

From the point of view of our objective of producing a criterion which would enable the EU to offer Lomé-equivalent GSP treatment to the non-least-developed ACP countries, the vulnerability index has the deficiency of being on a continuous scale, with values for the 110 countries studied ranging from 2.9 to 13.3, without providing a test of what is, and what is not, a statistically significant level of vulnerability. Given the range of values of the index, we have selected a value of 6.0 as the threshold level of significant vulnerability.

On this basis, 19 non-least-developed ACP countries would qualify for special treatment, including countries with a relatively high *per capita* GDP such as Mauritius. Conversely, 12 non-least-developed ACP countries would not be included: Congo, Barbados, Côte d'Ivoire, Nigeria, Trinidad and Tobago, Kenya, Senegal, Suriname, Cameroon, Zimbabwe, Ghana and Dominican Republic.

The development of the index is still at an experimental stage and further research is envisaged. For example, the dependent variables could take the form of the coefficient of variation rather than the standard deviation of the growth of *per capita* GDP. This would enable any variation in the growth rate to be expressed as a proportion of the average growth rate and would more accurately reflect the exposure of the economy to risk and uncertainty as well as enabling standard statistical tests of the significance of the index to be used. It is also unclear why the authors took the growth of *per capita* GDP rather than the growth of GDP as the dependent variable. The development of the index will not, however, necessarily assist the objectives of this study as the focus of the research is on the vulnerability of small developing countries and not the broader case for providing special preferences for the non-least-developed ACP.

An infant economy criterion

From the point of view of the objectives of this study, small size of population is simply a special case of the more general problems arising from the small size of the domestic market as a constraint on development. The confusion between the economic effects of a small size of population, and the problems of supplying a small market, are vividly illustrated by the example of Singapore. Singapore ranks fifth in the vulnerability index (out of 110 countries), but this does not reflect the fact that Singapore is economically disadvantaged but simply that it has a highly successful, export-oriented economy and therefore its generally high rate of growth varies according to the growth of world trade. A high exposure to world trade is a fundamental cause of the high rate of growth and economic development of the country, not a disadvantage.

The choice of 'small size' is also arbitrary, as there is no theoretical justification for any specific threshold. The size distribution of States is essentially continuous, and researchers have been unable to demonstrate that the effects of vulnerability are disproportionately intense below a particular size of population.

The fundamental case for providing trade preferences for developing countries is based on the infant industry, or more accurately the infant economy, argument. Countries with a small domestic market and relatively low level of economic development have to grow by entering into international trade at a relatively early stage in their economic development. But because of their state of underdevelopment they find it difficult to compete in world markets against well-established competitors. The sources of their lack of competitiveness are numerous and include the following:

❖ infant industry – which needs time both to move down the long-run average-cost curves to achieve minimum efficient scale of production and to 'learn by doing';

❖ infant economies – which lack a network of suppliers of intermediate goods and services;

❖ lack of attractiveness to import-substituting FDI – limiting the transfer of technology and knowledge about products, processes, and markets;

❖ external shocks which feed directly through the small economy and whose amplitude is not diminished by the complex system of input–output relationships found in a large economy; this increases risk and uncertainty and therefore reduces investment and growth.

These features are, of course, shared with developing countries with a small population. The difference between these countries and countries with a larger population is that the problem of vulnerability for the former will be long term and need appropriate solutions, whereas the problem for the latter is essentially transitory and will be removed with the process of economic development. Preferences were never envisaged as a permanent source of comparative advantage but simply as a short- to medium-term measure to overcome the disadvantages listed above, and so it is appropriate to develop a criterion which specifically seeks to isolate these key characteristics.

The constraints on economic development listed above can be identified in two sets of economies.

The first are economies that are small in terms of population and have a middle-income level of *per capita* GNP. These economies are vulnerable in the sense of the measures used by the vulnerability index. A small population, combined even with a middle-income level of *per capita* GNP, means that they have a small domestic market (as measured by GDP), but they have not reached a sufficient level of economic development (as measured by *per capita* GNP) to be able fully to overcome this constraint by relying on world trade for continued economic growth. A good example of such an economy is Mauritius, with one of the highest levels of *per capita* GNP of the ACP States, and which has been highly successful in using the trade preferences of Lomé. It is, however, a long way short of the level of economic development of a similar small economy such as Singapore, and fundamentally relies on exporting sugar and clothing. As discussed above, both of these products are subject to declining preferences and have an uncertain future and so Mauritius still requires trade preferences to enable it to overcome the constraints of its small domestic market and to diversify into a wider range of exports of goods and services.

The second group of countries is larger economies, in terms of size of population, but which have relatively low levels of *per capita* GNP. These economies are characterised by a larger size of domestic market than countries like Mauritius, but face similar problems in diversifying their exports because of their low levels of economic development. Examples of such economies include Kenya, Senegal, and Côte d'Ivoire. Within these limits will be a spectrum of economies with varying levels of GDP and *per capita* GNP.

If, for argument's sake, we set an upper limit on the first group of countries of a level of *per capita* GNP of $4,000 and GDP of $6,000 million, and a limit on the second group of economies of a level of *per capita* GNP of $700 and GDP of $11,000 million for the purposes of granting Lomé-equivalent preferences, then all of the ACP countries listed in the World Bank's *World Development Indicators 1998* would be covered, with the exceptions of Nigeria and the Dominican Republic. The only developing country to which such preferences would also have to be extended, and which is listed in the *World Development Indicators*, is Honduras. Some low-income Asian countries in the FSU would also qualify under these criteria, but these countries are not direct competitors with the ACP countries, and in any case the EU would probably wish to develop alternative trade relations with these countries. These criteria are purely illustrative, and would need to be rigorously developed in order to be put forward to the EU and accepted by the WTO, but they pass the basic tests of being 'plausible', 'simple to construct', 'suitable for international comparisons', and 'easily comprehended'.

With respect to improving to Lomé-equivalence the rules of origin, safeguard provisions and tolerance thresholds, it should be noted that the EU is committed to standardising the rules of origin for all of its preferential trade arrangements. It is therefore essential that the ACP ensure that this process is based on 'best practice', which, in most if not all cases, will require the application of the Lomé provisions to all beneficiaries as well as simplifying them for the least-developed countries.

The Way Ahead

This report is designed to provide background information to the ACP in preparing their negotiating position for the successor to the Lomé Convention. These negotiations are for a Framework Agreement, not for a REPA or any other non-Lomé trade regime. This is because the EU has agreed (subject to obtaining a WTO waiver) to extend Lomé access until 2005.

A key strategic question for the ACP, therefore, is to decide how detailed the Framework Agreement should be. There are arguments on both sides. A broad, general Framework Agreement has the advantage that it maximises the ACP's freedom of manoeuvre after Lomé has expired to shape any post-Lomé agreement (such as REPAs) to their best advantage. On the other hand, this freedom of manoeuvre applies

equally to the EU: a general Framework Agreement will not necessarily tie its hands and ensure a particular outcome. What would happen, for example, if the EU's initial contacts with important WTO members suggested to it, rightly or wrongly, that it would be difficult to obtain a waiver for the continuation of Lomé access?

The remainder of this section is based on the assumption that the ACP *may* wish to press for a detailed Framework Agreement. In the event that this assumption is incorrect, then no harm will have been done; the ACP can simply ignore the recommendations in this section.

The challenge facing the ACP is to negotiate an agreement (or set of agreements) over the next seven years that deals with the fact that:

❖ Lomé preferences are likely to be eroded over the next decade;

❖ the EU does not have 'off the peg' an alternative regime that is wholly satisfactory for the ACP and guaranteed to be immune to challenge in the WTO.

This report has argued that a sensible element of *any* negotiating strategy is to push for improvements to the GSP in order to provide a safety net. At the very least, this would reduce the danger of ACP countries being forced to negotiate under duress during any post-Lomé REPA talks.

If ACP States do decide to enter into REPA-style negotiations, then the examples of Morocco and South Africa provide a checklist of potential pitfalls of which they need to be aware. Whether or not a REPA makes economic and political sense for an ACP country cannot be determined until such negotiations have progressed. Their feasibility is also likely to be influenced by concurrent events, both regional and multilateral, that could influence trade policy.

Since there is no basis on which to speculate about the precise elements in any particular REPA or multilateral/regional changes that would affect particular ACP States, the Framework Agreement will need to be limited to more general provisions. These should aim to build upon Lomé's strengths. These are:

❖ Most fundamentally, its contractuality. This merit of Lomé supports several of the others, since it generates a feeling of security that, come what may, important elements of market access (or aid) cannot be removed at the whim of one side. It provides the confidence necessary for experimentation.

❖ Familiarity. This should not be underestimated. The A, the C and the P (not to mention anglophone and francophone Africans) have become used to dealing with each other and with the EU over 25 years. For all the difficulties that such co-operation engenders, it means that there is a familiarity on all sides with the key objectives and interests of the others that provides a sound foundation for policy development.

❖ A similarity of administrative and legal structures, given that most of the ACP have derived theirs from one of the European colonial models. This feature of the relationship will become increasingly important in the next century as the leading edge of trade policy reform increasingly involves harmonisation of legal and administrative codes.

❖ These features have given rise to a framework of trust, partly resulting from joint decision-making (despite the obvious imbalances in negotiating power) which has enabled Lomé to deal with such sensitive issues in the past as human rights and political conditionality more successfully than many bilateral accords.

The implications of building on these foundations can be summed up in a series of guiding principles. These should influence both what is in the Framework Agreement and the ways in which this is built upon subsequently. Recommendations are made in four broad areas in which specificity in the Framework Agreement could prove to be advantageous to the ACP. These are on regionalism, on special and differential treatment, on the new trade agenda and on global liberalisation.

ACP regionalism

It is desirable to ensure the continuation of ACP unity. Despite the difficulties of reaching agreement among 70 disparate States in three geographical regions, many cross-cutting relationships have been developed during the period of Lomés I–IV and these should be nurtured. It would be a great shame if the EU were deliberately to jettison one of its most remarkable creations.

The integration efforts that are emerging among ACP States should be supported. The lesson from this principle is that where integration is sufficiently advanced to permit a group of countries to negotiate jointly with the EU, and especially where the prospect of joint negotiations may strengthen the resolve to integrate, this can be very helpful. But ham-fisted and premature attempts to force the pace of integration in order to make things 'tidier' for the EU's benefit would be counter-productive.

Special and differential treatment

The EU should be persuaded to avoid the threat of a downgrading to the GSP to force ACP States to accept REPAs. The strategy will not work. It is probably an insufficiently strong and credible threat to force recalcitrant ACP States to sign up to a REPA. Whereas 'carrots' in the form of improved market access may sometimes help to overcome obstacles to liberalisation, 'sticks' in the form of threats to remove market access are less likely to be effective. But, even if the threat succeeds in persuading ACP States to sign up to the letter of REPAs, it will not force them to accept the spirit of them. Under the EU's current proposals, ACP liberalisation will be delayed until the end of the transitional period. As explained above, by this time a large part of the value of current market access will have disappeared, as a result of broader EU liberalisation. Hence, there will be very little stimulus for ACP members of REPAs actually to implement their commitments to lower barriers on sensitive products by the time this is demanded of them.

The new-found concern to forge a joint EU–ACP caucus within the WTO should be used. It is very likely that the next ten years will see a host of WTO negotiations which may profoundly affect ACP, and other developing, States. A key feature of the WTO is that it combines voting equality with a considerable inequality of negotiating resources. Most (if not all) ACP States will be unable to monitor all the fora in which their interests are at stake, and so effective operation in the WTO requires them to network and co-ordinate. If it were possible to establish common interests between the EU and the ACP, this would be of considerable negotiating benefit to the ACP, and a not insignificant gain for the EU. There exists a reason to anticipate, therefore, that mutual self-interest could be advanced in this way. But there must be a common agreement on what is to be done, or else the benefits of collaboration will not flow.

New trade issues

The Framework Agreement should not be used as a blunt instrument to force onto ACP States new, highly contentious issues of trade policy (particularly in the areas of TRIPs, TRIMs and services) for which multilateral agreement is absent, the benefits for ACP States are questionable and the desirability of proceeding in a sub-multilateral fashion is suspect.

The ACP may wish, however, to advance the process of agreeing rules in the new areas of trade policy where this can more conveniently be done within the post-Lomé framework at a multilateral level. There are a number of areas in which such progress could be possible.

First, the similarity of legal and administrative systems in the EU and ACP, and the more sympathetic approach to questions of special and differential treatment for poor and vulnerable countries exhibited by the EU (compared, for example, with the USA), mean that it may be possible to establish principles that could then be used as a standard against which multilateral discussions should be judged. One example would be in the definition of the adequacy of *sui generis* approaches to the protection of intellectual property rights in plants. This is likely to be a highly contentious area in the future, and any success in the EU–ACP forum in establishing a workable set of criteria would place the group in a good position to influence the wider debate in the WTO.

Second, the new concern with international regulation on, for example, the protection of origin denomination, may provide an opportunity to exchange ACP acceptance of EU origin marques (such as on the definition of champagne, sherry and port) with EU acceptance of long-held ACP positions on products of importance to the group. This would be of importance, for example, to rum.

Third, it may be possible to make advances within the post-Lomé framework on a code for handling the new areas of trade policy that are, effectively, tariff substitutes. These include the misuse of anti-dumping operations, as well as the threat of safeguard action. Given the growing willingness of developing countries to impose anti-dumping duties on EU agricultural exports, there could be a basis for establishing a code of conduct for both sides in the application of anti-dumping actions. This could then be translated into a proposal in the multilateral forum for future discussion.

Preparing for a more liberal world

The ACP should use all the provisions of the successor Convention to help their economies to adapt to a new, more liberalised world economy. There is a great deal to be done. Priority areas include:

❖ Increasing production of items which are likely to become more scarce/higher-priced in a liberalised world (such as basic staple foods).

❖ Reducing the cost of production of items for which European prices are likely to fall (including sugar, beef and horticultural products), as well as improving and reducing the cost of transport services.

❖ Improving ACP capacity to adhere to the phytosanitary and other standards and procedures that are increasingly required in high-price markets. Such standards are likely to rise, regardless of the formal provisions within trade policy, as consumers become more health conscious and retailers adapt their buying policies to take account of this. Increasingly, countries that do not have locally based certification laboratories, approved by the health authorities in important export markets, will find themselves unable to export to those markets, or at least to the premium sub-markets. This may require a great deal of investment (capital and human) to establish such facilities.

❖ Help to adjust to an era in which trade taxes yield much lower levels of government revenue. Such adjustment must include establishing alternative means of revenue raising (which will be difficult and time consuming, precisely because trade taxes are usually the easiest source of government revenue) and establishing new patterns of government expenditure that take account of the, probably, lower relative levels of public revenue in the future.

These suggestions are in addition to any proposals on which the ACP may agree concerning, for example, what has been called 'a third option' (i.e. an alternative to REPAs and the GSP). It would make considerable sense for the ACP to identify and promote such an option (or options), given that neither the GSP nor the REPA option is wholly satisfactory. Technical support for developing the details of such option(s) could be appropriate and feasible.

However, this report has not proposed any detailed third option. This is because technical analysis is the second stage in the development of an option. The first stage, which is political, has not yet been completed by the ACP. It is to identify and agree upon one of the many potential options that can be envisaged.

In the absence of this political agreement, the report has limited itself to identifying the challenges facing the ACP in the current negotiations and thereafter, and to proposing a set of tactics to deal with them. These tactics are designed to be 'strategy neutral'. In other words, they are compatible with any broader strategy that the ACP may adopt now or in the future – as a group, as sub-regions, or as individual States. The aim has been to maximise the ACP's freedom of manoeuvre in making or following through the Framework Agreement whilst at the same time limiting the EU's ability to walk away from its current commitments on trade.

References

Atkins, J., Mazzi, J. and Ramlogan, C. (1998). *A Study of the Vulnerability of Developing and Island States: A Composite Index*. London: Commonwealth Secretariat.

Baughman, L., Mirus, R., Morkre, M.E. and Spinanger, D. (1997). 'Of Tyre Cords, Ties and Tents: Window Dressing in the ATC?'. *World Economy* 20(4): 407–34.

Bhagwati, J. and Panagariya, A. (1996). *The Economics of Preferential Trade Agreements*. Washington DC: AEI Press.

Croome, J. (1995). *Reshaping the World Trading System: A History of the Uruguay Round*. Geneva: World Trade Organization.

EU Council (1998). 'Negotiating directives for the negotiation of a development partnership agreement with the ACP counties'. Information Note 10017/98. Brussels: European Union, The Council (30 June).

Eurostat (1996).*Intra- and extra-EU trade (annual data – Combined Nomenclature)*. Supplement 2 1996 (CD-Rom). Luxembourg: Statistical Office of the European Communities.

Eurostat (1997).*Intra- and extra-EU trade (annual data – Combined Nomenclature)*. Supplement 2 1997 (CD-Rom). Luxembourg: Statistical Office of the European Communities.

GATT (1947). *The General Agreement on Tariffs and Trade*. In WTO, *op. cit.*

GSP (1994). 'Council Regulation (EC) No 3281/94 of 19 December 1994 applying a four-year scheme of generalized tariff preferences (1995 to 1998) in respect of certain industrial products originating in developing countries'. *Official Journal of the European Communities, L 348*. 37 (31 December 1994; subsequent corrigenda/amendments in *L 82* (12 April 1995), *L 177* (24 May 1995), *L 208* (5 September 1995) and *L 97* (18 April 1996). Luxembourg: Office for Official Publications of the European Communities.

GSP (1996). 'Council Regulation (EC) No 1256/96 of 20 June 1996 applying multiannual schemes of generalized tariff preferences from 1 July 1996 to 30 June 1999 in respect of certain agricultural products originating in developing countries'. *Official Journal of the European Communities, L 160*. 39 (29 June 1996), and subsequent corrigendum in *L 152* (11 June 1997). Luxembourg: Office for Official Publications of the European Communities.

Hertel, T., Martin, W., Yanagishima, K. and Dimaranan, B. (1996). 'Liberalizing Manufactures Trade in a Changing World Economy'. In Martin, W. and Winters, L. A. (eds).*The Uruguay Round and the Developing Countries*.. Cambridge: Cambridge University Press.

Kennan, J. and Stevens, C. (1997). 'From Lomé to the GSP: Implications for the ACP of Losing Lomé Trade Preferences'. Report prepared for Oxfam UK. Brighton: Institute of Development Studies.

Taric 1996. 'Integrated tariff of the European Communities (Taric)' (4 volumes), *Official Journal of the European Communities C 98 A*, Volume 39, 1 April 1996. Luxembourg: Office for Official Publications of the European Communities.

Wonnacott, R.J. 1996. 'Trade and Investment in a Hub-and-Spoke System Versus a Free Trade Area', *The World Economy*, 19(3): 237–52.

Wonnacott, P. and Lutz, M., 1989. 'Is there a case for free trade areas?', in Schott, J.J. (ed.), *Free Trade Areas and US Trade Policy*. Washington DC: Institute for International Economics.

World Bank 1996. *Growing Faster, Finding Jobs: Choices for Morocco*. Washington DC: The World Bank (August).

WTO 1995. *The Results of the Uruguay Round of Multilateral Trade Negotiations: The Legal Texts*. Geneva: The World Trade Organization.

WTO 1996. *The Results of the Uruguay Round* (CD-Rom). Geneva: World Trade Organization.

Recent Commonwealth Secretariat Economic Publications

Commonwealth Economic Papers

Graham Bird and Tony Killick, *The Bretton Woods Institutions: A Commonwealth Perspective*, No.24, 1996

David Greenway and Chris Milner, *The Uruguay Round and Developing Countries: An Assessment*, No.25, 1996

Michael Davenport, *The Uruguay Round and NAFTA: The Challenge for Commonwealth Caribbean Countries*, No.26, 1996

Economic Affairs Division, *Money Laundering: Key Issues and Possible* Action, No.27, 1997

David Pearce and Ece Ozdemiroglu, *Integrating the Economy and the Environment – Policy and Practice*, No.28, 1997

Robert Cassen, *Strategies for Growth and Poverty Alleviation*, No.29, 1997

Richard Portes and David Vines, *Coping with International Capital Flows*, No.30, 1997

Sanjaya Lall, *Attracting Foreign Direct Investment*, No.31, 1997

M. McQueen, C. Phillips, D. Hallam & A.Swinbank, *ACP-EU Trade and Aid Co-operation Post-Lomé IV*, No.32, 1998

Sanjaya Lall and Ganeshan Wignaraja, *Mauritius: Dynamising Export Competitiveness* , No.33, 1998.

Report of a Commonwealth Working Group, *Promoting Private Capital Flows and Handling Volatility:Role of National and International Policies*, No.34, 1998

Gerry K Helleiner, Private Capital Flows and Development: *The Role of National and International Policies*, No.35, 1998

Joseph LS Abbey, *The Political Process and Management of Economic Change*, No.36, 1998

Alan Swinbank, Kate Jordan and Nick Beard, *Implications for Developing Countries of likely Reforms of the Common Agricultural Policy of the Europena Union*, No.38, 2000

Sanjaya Lall, *Promoting Industrial Competitiveness in Developing Countries: Lessons from Asia*, No.39, 1999

Jonathan Atkins, Sonia Mazzi and Christopher Easter, A *Commonwealth Vulnerability Index for Developing Countries: The Position of Small States*, No.40, 2000

To order these or any other publication, please contact:
Publication Unit, Commonwealth Secretariat
Marlborough House, Pall Mall, London SW1Y 5HX, United Kingdom.
Tel: +44 (0)20 7747 6342; or Fax: +44 (0)20 7839 9081